DNA Science and the Jewish Bloodline

RiverCrest Publishing
1708 Patterson Road • Austin, Texas 78733

ACKNOWLEDGEMENTS

My staff deserves maximum praise for their outstanding contributions. Included: Michelle Powell, business administrator, Sandra Myers, publishing and art; Jerry Barrett, computer and internet manager; Rosario Velasquez, shipping manager; and Nelson Sorto, shipping department. To my wife and confidant, Wanda Marrs, goes all my love and gratefulness.

DNA Science and the Jewish Bloodline

Second Printing, 2015

Portions of this book were previously published by Texe Marrs and RiverCrest Publishing.

All Scripture quotations are from the King James Version of The Holy Bible.

Cover design: Sandra Myers

Printed in the United States of America

Library of Congress Catalog Card Number 2013909753

Categories:	1. Religion	2. Judaism
	3. Science	4. History
	5. Archaeology	

ISBN 978-1-930004-81-8

Martin Luther on the Jews

"No one can take away from them their pride concerning their blood and their descent from Israel… All the prophets censored them for it, for it betrays an arrogant, carnal presumption devoid of spirit and faith. Our Lord also calls them a "brood of vipers;" furthermore, in John 8:39, 44 he states: "If ye were Abraham's children ye would do the works of Abraham… Ye are of your father the devil." It was intolerable to them to hear that they were not Abraham's but the devil's children, nor can they bear to hear this today. If they should surrender this boast and argument, their whole system which is built on it would topple and change."

OTHER BOOKS BY TEXE MARRS

Robot Alchemy: Androids, Cyborgs, and the Magic of Artificial Life

Conspiracy of the Six-Pointed Star

Conspiracy World

Mysterious Monuments: Encyclopedia of Secret Illuminati Designs, Masonic Architecture, and Occult Places

Codex Magica: Secret Signs, Mysterious Symbols and Hidden Codes of the Illuminati

Days of Hunger, Days of Chaos: The Coming Great Food Shortages in America

Project L.U.C.I.D.: The Beast 666 Universal Human Control System

Circle of Intrigue: The Hidden Inner Circle of the Global Illuminati Conspiracy

Dark Majesty: The Secret Brotherhood and the Magic of a Thousand Points of Light

New Age Cults and Religions

Mystery Mark of the New Age: Satan's Design for World Domination

Dark Secrets of the New Age: Satan's One World Plan for Domination

For additional information we highly recommend the following websites:

www.powerofprophecy.com
www.conspiracyworld.com

T A B L E   O F
Contents

INTRODUCTION

"And If Ye Be Christ's, Then Are Ye Abraham's Seed"

Definitive DNA studies have now been conducted, and the results are clear and indisputable. The people who today call themselves "Jews" and reside both in the Middle East and around the world are not descendants of the ancient Israelites. They are not the seed of Abraham and have no blood connection to the prophets of ancient Israel. Instead, DNA shows these people to be descendants of the Kingdom of Khazaria, a country that formerly existed in the Caucasus, south of Russia.

History records that in the 8th century the King of Khazaria chose Judaism as the preferred religion for his people, who at that time were pagans and nativists. He ordered that Jewish rabbis be brought into Khazaria from Babylon to teach his people of this new religion.

The people of Khazaria were conquered over the next two centuries by Russian invaders. Many fled to Eastern Europe, principally to Poland, where they retained their Judaic religion. From there they emigrated throughout Europe and into the United States and, in 1948, the Khazarian Jews established the new nation of Israel.

Those people throughout the world who today refer to themselves as "Jews" are actually Khazarians, and of Turkish/ Mongol stock. They erroneously believe themselves to be ancient Israelites, but, in fact, are Gentiles. Many practice the religion of Judaism, and their Babylonian Talmud claims that the Jews are a superior, god-like race. Ironically, the Talmud states that the Gentiles are inferior, being no more than cattle (the *goyim*). The Talmud also speaks of "Israel" as being the eternal homeland for the Jews and of a Jewish Messiah to come and rule the world.

The persistence of the Khazarians to insist they are "Jews" and their Talmudic doctrines have resulted in conflict and division wherever they have resided. This is especially true in Israel, a land where native-born Palestinians, most of whom are Moslems, also have territorial claims.

Paul, in the New Testament, told us to beware of those who emphasize race and national origins. He spoke of *"foolish genealogies."* God's children, however, are born again in spirit and in truth *(John 3:3).*

God surely confounds those who are the "children of pride," who hold that their race and blood is superior to that of their fellow human beings. That is clearly why he has surprised us with His mathematical certainty through DNA science that, in fact, almost all of the "Jews" today in the world are Khazars. They are not the seed of Abraham nor his physical heirs. They have no physical or family ties with Abraham and the prophets.

This seems at first glance to be a tragedy for the Jews, whose human pride is damaged at the revelation that they are not "God's Chosen" and not so special after all. It also sends the whole world a clear signal that the land of Israel does *not* belong to the "Jews" for they are Khazars and their national homeland is not Israel, but Khazaria, in the Caucasus.

But what at first seems bad news, even a disaster for the Khazar Jew, becomes, in fact, a marvelous opportunity. Now the "Jew" is free from the burden to create an Israeli homeland. He can bid farewell to his exclusion from the rest of humanity and thereby rejoin the human race.

God's Word shows the way to life through faith in Jesus Christ. My prayer is that Christians will avail themselves of this opportunity to bless the Khazars and to witness to them of the love of Jesus. For only in this way can the Khazar truly be free and know liberty. As is recorded in the scriptures, in *Galatians 3:26-29*:

> *"For ye are all the children of God by faith in Christ Jesus.*
>
> *For as many of you as have been baptized into Christ have put on Christ.*
>
> *There is neither Jew nor Greek, there is neither bond nor free, there is neither male nor female: for ye are all one in Christ Jesus.*
>
> *And if ye be Christ's, then are ye Abraham's seed, and heirs according to the Promise."*

— Texe Marrs
Austin, Texas

ONE

DNA Science and the Jewish Bloodline

"And the Lord appeared unto Abram, and said,
Unto thy seed will I give this land…"
—*Genesis 12:7*

There is absolutely no doubt that God made a covenant with Abraham. Under this covenant, Abram and his seed were promised a great swath of land we today call Israel, but also partially encompassing land in the current nations of Lebanon, Syria, Egypt, and Iraq. We can call this territory *"Greater Israel."*

This covenant was confirmed by God when he led the Jews out of the land of Egypt. That is when he again promised them the land of Israel, and He kept His promise.

The great controversy, however, involves the question of whether or not this covenant is still operative and in place today. My own view is that it is not. God surely made this covenant and He kept his end of the bargain. Unfortunately, Israel did not. They abrogated—terminated—the covenant by their sin and evil conduct.

A New and Better Covenant

This voiding of the old covenant is recorded in the New Testament's book of Hebrews in which the Apostle Paul explains that Jesus is the mediator of a *new and better covenant:*

> *"But now hath he obtained a more excellent ministry, by how much he also is mediator of a better covenant, which can be established upon better promises.*
>
> *For if that first covenant had been faultless, then there should no place have been sought for the second.*
>
> *In that he saith, A new covenant, he hath made the first old. Now that which decayeth and waxeth old is ready to vanish away." (Hebrews 8:6-7, 13)*

The new and better covenant is deposited and is alive in Jesus Christ and it is offered to all the nations through faith (see *Hebrews 11*). Thus, the people of faith, Jew and Gentile, seek not a Holy City here on earth, but a heavenly one. That is the wonderful promise of God to His chosen people, Christians who have faith:

> *"But now they desire a better country, that is, an heavenly: wherefore God is not ashamed to be called their God: for he hath prepared for them a city." (Hebrews 11:16)*

Abraham, Isaac, Jacob, Moses, all the patriarchs, prophets

and saints, having been saved *not* by the law but by their faith in God and His Son, are now in heaven *(Hebrews 12:22-24)*. That is the glory promised, the heavenly city of Jerusalem, that awaits all people of faith.

> *"Looking unto Jesus the author and finisher of our faith: who for the joy that was set before him endured the cross...is set down at the right hand of the throne of God."*

Jews and Gentiles in the New Covenant

Therefore, a remnant of Jews shall be saved, we are told, and they shall become one with the saints of God, for Abraham's seed is one, Christ Jesus *(Galatians 3:16)*, not the many of the physical state of Israel.

> *"And if ye be Christ's, then are ye Abraham's seed, and heirs according to the promise." (Galatians 3:29)*

The good news, then, is that it does not matter what your race or national origin. Faith is inclusive—all may come through faith: "For ye are all the children of God by faith in Christ Jesus...There is neither Jew nor Greek, there is neither bond nor free, there is neither male or female: for ye are all one in Christ Jesus" *(Galatians 3:26-28)*.

Thus, God's kingdom is made up of all races and national origins. He is a God of love. He is not a racist but, instead, loves all and wants people everywhere to believe in His Son and be saved.

Christian Zionists Continue to Profess the Old Covenant

Yet, there is a contingent in Christianity who reject these clear principles. They have separated one people, one nation from the rest and proclaimed that nation and that only as "God's Chosen." Yes, this contingent claims that God never abrogated the old covenant. They say that the Jews remain God's "eternal people."

Now there are many in this contingent so extreme in their views that the Jews become like "little gods." The old covenant, they say, still applies and the Jews, they maintain, do not need Jesus for salvation. They need only to obey the 613 laws of Judaism (the *Halacha*).

This "two covenant" belief is today spreading like wildfire, especially among those who   proclaim themselves to be "Christian Zionists."

Whatever view the Christian Zionist takes toward Israel, it is for certain that *every* Christian Zionist essentially believes that: (1) God has *separated* the Jews and the Christians; (2) God has a *separate* plan for the Jews; and (3) God desires that every Jew *return* to Israel.

Some Christian Zionists—the Messianics—actually have synagogues. They have men called "rabbis" who lead their assemblies; they observe the festivals of Judaism; and they obey many of the laws of Judaism.

Only Jews Possess the Land?

The major, abiding principle of the Christian Zionists (the Bible calls them "Judaizers") is their insistence that the land of Israel in the Middle East belongs only to the Jews. Since the Abrahamic covenant is still operative in their view, then the seed of Abraham has "title" to the land.

This "land principle" is a vital part of the Christian Zionist belief system, and their political power insures that the "Jews" in Israel today not only possess much of the land, but are annually given billions of dollars in foreign aid by the U.S.

Over the years, some $2 trillion has been given to the nation of Israel, plus billions of dollars in military armaments. According to the Christian Zionists, this support of Israel and the Jews is a mandatory requirement of God. Those who bless Israel will be blessed, and those who do not are cursed. By their firm, even fanatical, support of Israel, the Zionist believes he is doing God's will.

What This Book Covers

In this book, we first examine the DNA science which now reveals to all who are the Jews of Israel and the world. Only the descendants of Abraham—bloodline Jews, say the Christian Zionists—are entitled to "Chosen" status and to the land first promised their ancient father, Abraham, some 5,000 years ago.

Are the modern-day Jews the *descendants* of Abraham? Are they his *seed?* DNA science gives us the answer, and history and archeology provide strong support.

We will also examine the scriptural basis of the Christian Zionist contingent and determine the authenticity of their claims. It is true that the Old Testament promised Abraham and his seed the land. But what does the New Testament say? Was God's promise actually fulfilled?

Finally, we will take a look at Khazaria, that mysterious yet real nation of the Caucasus (southern Russia). Is this once great nation the origin of today's "Jews?" Are the Jews of Israel and the Diaspora authentic, pure racial Jews, of the bloodline of their Israelite ancestors? Or, are they imposters?

TWO

The Evidence is Clear— Today's Jews are Khazars

"This new study *(Elhaik, "The Missing Link of Jewish European Ancestry: Contrasting the Rhineland and Khazarian Hypotheses," Genome Biology and Evolution, December 2012)* supports the theory that the Jews are descendants of different peoples who converted to Judaism...The dominant element in the genetic makeup is Khazar."
— "The Jewish People's
Ultimate Treasure Hunt,"
Haaretz newspaper, pp 1-15

Are you a Christian Zionist? Do you believe that the people of Israel, the Jews, are eternally God's Chosen People?

Do you believe, moreover, that God wants all the Jews in the world to return to the nation of Israel and make their residence?...that God gave the land only to the Jews through their father, Abraham?…that it is their land forever?

Do you believe, too, that all who bless the Jews will be blessed by God, and those who curse the Jews will be cursed by God?

As a Christian Zionist, do you believe that today's Jews are descendants of Abraham, Isaac, and Jacob…that they are the very seed of Abraham?

If you believe these things, then this book is definitely for you. You need to know about DNA science and its relationship to the Jewish bloodline because it is this science that can confirm for you who *are* Jews and who *are not* Jews.

Why is this important to you? Well, if a man comes up to you and says, *"I am a Jew,"* how do you know he's telling the truth? What if he tells you *"I am a Jew and I want to go to Israel?"*

What if this man then says, *"The land of Israel belongs to me and to my race, but another people, the Palestinians, are now living in my home in Israel. Please help me take back my home."*

Would you do it? Would you help him? Surely, you would want first to know if he is who he says he is, that he's really a Jew. If he's *not* a Jew, he doesn't get the land, does he? And if he is a racial imposter, then he does not deserve your support, right? If the man is actually say, a Japanese, Chinese, or African, you would legitimately say, "Hey, you're *not* a Jew! You're an imposter. Get out of here!"

Certainly, no one would blame you for denying the man your help, your support, if he really were not a Jew.

The point is, Christian Zionists believe that Israel is only for real Jews, descendants of Abraham, Jews of the bloodline of Abraham, Jews who are of the twelve tribes, mentioned in the book of *Revelation*. You know that this Japanese (or Chinese, or African) does not look like a Jew, but can you be sure he's not what he claims? The question is, how can you know for sure whether the man is or is not a Jew?

DNA Science Provides Irrefutable Evidence

Well, the very best method of determining one's race is to test their DNA. In 1968, British scientists Crick and Watson scientifically established that every human being has DNA traits that identify exactly their origins. It's simple, and DNA is virtually 100% scientifically accurate.

No question about it. Since DNA became available, hundreds of thousands of people around the world have been tested. The courts use DNA all the time to either catch a criminal, or perhaps to exonerate the innocent. Without DNA, many criminal cases would never be solved.

DNA is also used to establish who is the birth father or mother of a newborn baby—or an adult. It is useful in civil courts across the globe to affix birth and adjudge cases.

Thanks to DNA, scientists and other researchers are now able to determine the race, tribe, or ethnic group to which a person, or even an entire nation, belongs. In fact this is the proper use of DNA in the case we are now discussing—that of the man claiming to be Jewish.

Simply test the man's DNA and you can definitely tell if he *is* a Jew, or is an imposter. Of course, there are other ways to check a person's race and ethnic group, but none except DNA are perfect.

Many people claim to be what they are not due to advantage. It often pays to be a Native American, a black, a Mexican, or another race.

So you test the individual's DNA and the results come back. No, the man is *not* a Jew, he's (surprise) a Samoan, a Fiji Islander, or of some other race. But he's definitely not a Jew. He's not of Israelite stock. He is not the seed of Abraham, and he has no right to settle in Israel. Nor does he, as an imposter, have a right to the land.

After all, as a Christian Zionist, you believe, do you not, that Israel is only for Jews? God gave their father, Abraham, the title to the land over 5,000 years ago?

Are the People Living in Israel Today Genetic Jews?

Now keeping these facts in mind, how do you know if the people who now live in Israel are, in fact, really Jews? It has only been since 1948 that Israel has been an independent nation. How do you know if the people who live there are descendants of Abraham, his seed. It is important for Christian Zionists to know whether people come from the true and legitimate Jewish bloodline.

For that matter, what of the Jews here in America? How do you really know they are Jews? Do you simply trust what they say they are?

Don't you wish you had someone who could give all the Jews in the world a DNA test? After all, it is certainly not right for Christian Zionists to give fakes and imposters things that God intends only for Jews, right?

DNA Tests Tell the Story

Well, good news! DNA tests *have essentially already been conducted* on those who say they are Jews. The results are *in!* Are you ready to discover now what modern DNA science has to say about the people who claim to be God's Chosen?

Scientific DNA studies were conducted first in 2001 by Dr. Ariella Oppenheim, a Jewish genetics researcher of Hebrew University in Tel Aviv. Her finding: Almost all who today identify themselves as "Jews" are *not* the descendants of Abraham but are, in fact, of Turkish/Mongol stock. The Jews are Khazarians, not Israelites.

Then, in 2012, Dr. Eran Elhaik, an Israeli-born, Jewish researcher from prestigious Johns Hopkins Medical University in Baltimore, Maryland, published his findings. They confirmed those of Oppenheim: Those who today identify themselves as "Jews" are *not* the descendants of Abraham but are, in fact, of Turkish/Mongol stock. The Jews are Khazarians, not Israelites.

According to Dr. Elhaik's research, those who identify themselves as today's Jew and as descendants, therefore, of Abraham, are mistaken. They actually can be traced back to Khazaria. There, in the 8th century, the people of Khazaria converted to Judaism. As reporter Ofer Aderat states in Israel's newspaper, *Haaretz*:

"…the Khazars converted to Judaism in the eighth century and their descendants are the "European" or "Ashkenazi" Jews who live today in Israel and the Diaspora…The commonly accepted narrative consider the Jews to be descended from the residents of the Kingdom of Judah who were exiled and returned to their native land—the modern-day State of Israel—only after thousands of years of exile. In contrast, this new study *(Elhaik, "The Missing Link of Jewish European Ancestry: Contrasting the Rhineland and Khazarian Hypotheses," Genome Biology and Evolution, December 2012)* supports the theory that the Jews are descendants of different peoples who converted to Judaism…The dominant element in the genetic makeup is Khazar."

"The Jewish People's
Ultimate Treasure Hunt,"
Haaretz newspaper, pp 1-15

Khazars Not Family Related to Jews or Israel

The Khazarians at the time had absolutely no family relationship with the Jews or with Israel. They were pagans into nature and phallus worship. But their King (called *Kagan*) Bulan decided his entire country of Khazaria would convert to Judaism, and many Khazarians became "Jews" through conversion.

It is, of course, one thing for the Khazarian people to become Jews and to learn and practice the religion of Judaism. It is, however, quite another for a people to be *descendants* of the bloodline of Abraham. Moreover, these new converts had never set foot in Israel which, at that time, was under the heel of the Moslems.

Within a few hundred years, Khazaria, which at one time had been the largest state in either Asia or Europe, had been defeated by Russian forces. Khazaria fell under the domination of the Russians. Many Khazarians left and emigrated eastward, into Poland and Lithuania. There, the Khazars settled as "Jews" and kept their adopted religion, Judaism.

Over time, the Khazars drifted on into other European nations, into Romania, Austria, France, and Germany, etc. Most forgot where they had originally come from and even that they were Khazars. They simply knew that they were "Jews" and identified themselves as Jews.

More on the Khazars and their once, great nation of Khazaria later in this book. But for now, I would like to reiterate the *fact* that these Khazars called themselves "Jews" and over time, most forgot their origins. Some of these supposed Jews—actually Khazars—finally emigrated from Europe to America beginning about 1890 and on into the 1920s. Then, in the years after World War II, many Khazar Jews left Europe and sought refuge in Palestine which became Israel in 1948.

Today, demographers report there are approximately 7.5

million who identify as Jews in the U.S.A. In Israel we find another 7.5 million and there are some 3 million Jews in Europe and elsewhere in the world.

The vast majority of these 18 million "Jews" are Khazars, as the DNA research of Elhaik, Oppenheim, and others document. Nowhere in all the world has there been found a man or woman who can say, with veracity, *"I am of the same race as my father Abraham."*

Let me repeat, nowhere is there a human being alive who can prove he or she is authentic, DNA proven Israelite, a descendant of Abraham.

There is no such thing, anywhere in the world, as a race of Jews. Even the *Encyclopedia Judaica* acknowledges this fact.

No Jewish Exile

It was thought by Christians that the majority of the Jews, driven from Jerusalem by Roman General Titus in 70 AD, had emigrated to Rome and to Europe, particularly Germany, and then on into Eastern Europe. The theory was that the Jews who resided and then became the Diaspora in Europe were Middle East exiles.

But historians and archaeologists disputed this account. Most said that after Titus, only a few of the Jews were dispersed throughout the Roman world. They intermarried with the local peoples and, essentially, were dissolved as a homogenous race. However, most of the Jews remained in the Middle East, grouping themselves in Babylon and other locales in close-knit communities, cleaving together under their rabbis and continuing their practice of Judaism.

The Jewish leaders hotly disputed the accounts of the historians and archaeologists. They insisted that the Jews, being Middle East exiles, had settled first in Europe as Jews, then finally emigrated elsewhere. It was essential for the rabbis and other Jewish leaders to maintain this fiction. With this myth, they could maintain that they were, indeed, descendants of Abraham, his seed, and had retained their bloodline.

Myth of a Pure Race

With this Jewish myth of Middle East origin intact, the Jews could proclaim themselves to be a "pure race." They could continue their claim to the land God had given Abraham in Genesis. The Jews could also trumpet they would eventually "return" to Israel, that it was an "eternal" possession of the Jews, that as His chosen people God had given them the title through Abraham.

"Next year, Jerusalem" became the rallying cry for the people who called themselves Jews.

But, if these people had only been "Jews" since the 8th century, if they had converted to Judaism, pressed to do so by their King Bulan, if indeed the Jews were Khazarians and not Israelites, everything changes.

In that case, the Jews had no legitimate claim on the land of Israel. They had no Israelite ancestors. Indeed, the ancestors of the Khazarians had never been in Israel, never set foot on holy soil. The Khazar "Jews" were taught their Judaic religion by rabbis exported by King Bulan from nearby Babylon beginning in the 8th century. All they knew of Israel had been told to them.

The Khazars Could Not "Return" to Israel

As Khazars it was impossible for the "Jews" to *return* to Israel, a place they and their ancestors had never been. Their genetic roots were in the Caucasus, in what became Southern Russia, and the people of Khazaria were mainly of Turkish stock. They had no blood or family ties to Israel. Thus, the claim to Jewish extraction was a hollow claim. It was as if a group of

Japanese laid claim to being originally from South America and declared that Rio de Janeiro and Brazil was their eternal possession.

In that case, the indigenous people of Rio de Janeiro and Brazil would be quite upset if, in 1948, the Japanese emigrated *enmasse* and set up a new nation. If, then, the Brazilians were uprooted from their homes, businesses, farms, and killed and persecuted by the Japanese contingent would not there be fierce resistance?

Would *you* allow an outside group with no real connection to your homeland to come in and seize *your* property, claiming it as their possession because, they say, God gave it to their ancestors 5,000 years ago?

Plight of the Palestinians

In this perspective, we can well understand the argument and plight of the native Palestinians. They were the majority, and they had lived in their homeland for centuries, building homes, planting orchards, and setting up shops and businesses. They generally had lived in peace, owning no firearms or weapons and having no military to protect them from attack. Suddenly, in 1900, the Jews (Khazars) began to descend on their peaceful territory, claiming title to what was clearly the territories of the Palestinians.

This outside force of Khazar "Jews" naturally met resistance, this especially being true because most of the native-born Palestinians were Moslems, whereas the "invaders," the Khazar "Jews," claimed to be Judaic.

We see already in the United States the ongoing bitterness and conflict caused in the recent past by the arrival of Moslem immigrants into our country. Applied to Palestine, we can multiply this anger and resentment. In Palestine, the Jews, believing themselves an entitled "super race," not only began to discriminate against and persecute the indigenous peoples (Moslem Palestinians), but made clear that they, the Palestinians, were their inferiors.

The arriving Jews (actually, *Khazars*) made the new nation of Palestine (or, *Israel*) a Jewish state. They passed laws forbidding Palestinians the right to vote and the right to own land, and they discriminated against them in many other aspects as well.

For those Palestinians who had fled the Israeli invasion in 1948, things were particularly brutal and harsh. The Jews legislated that the Palestinian natives could *not* return to their homeland. Thus, they became permanent outcasts, forced to survive in primitive tent communities in the hostile desert. This kind of treatment must, of necessity, breed resentment and stir up anger in the hearts of those affected.

Dear Christian, put yourself in the Palestinians' shoes. Would *you* also, if these things happened to you here in the United States, be bitter? Would you not seek recompense for all the indignities heaped on you and for the stealing of your property?

It is not only the Palestinian Moslems who have suffered. Many of the native-born Palestinians are *Christian*. These Christians also have been uprooted and have become objects of hate and discrimination by the Jews.

The Crux of the Matter

The crux of the matter is that Khazar people—who are not blood Jews—wanted the land of Israel for their possession, and thanks to Americans, they have seized and now are using brutal methods to control the native-born Palestinians. Is this okay with Christians?

Is the title to Israel the right of converted "Jews"—really Gentiles—who are not the descendants of Abraham? That is the question. And if anyone can convert to Judaism, does that conversion mean that, presto!, the convert immediately has the Abrahamic Covenant?

Celebrities and Movie Stars Become Jews

Marilyn Monroe, Sammy Davis, Jr.—they were Gentiles who converted to Judaism. Are you, Zionist Christian, willing to say that these Hollywood types thereby *owned* the title to Israel and were entitled to the promise of Abraham?

In recent years, the following celebrities—movie and TV stars, politicians, newsmen, etc.—proved their "Jewishness" by study of the Jewish Kabbala. Most were born Gentile. They wear the red wristband signifying they are believers in the Kabbalah. They recited the *Ona Be' Kaach* and the *Bon Porat* Jewish prayers. Are these people entitled to all the promises given father Abraham? Is the title to the land of Israel given to

Many movie stars—including Marilyn Monroe and Sammy Davis, Jr.—have converted to Judaism. Should converts be given the land?

converts or is it reserved strictly for the seed of Abraham?

Nicole Richy
Paris Hilton
Bill Clinton
Britney Spears
Mick Jagger
Madonna
"Posh" Beckham
Stephen Colbert
John Kerry
Zac Efron
Billie Piper
Lindsey Lohan
Teri Hatcher
Brian Williams
Demi Moore

A Colossal Hoax

If it is the *seed of Abraham*, the Jewish bloodline, that has the promise, then neither these people nor the whole Jewish world—including almost the entire nation of Israel—are qualified to own the land of Israel.

If God chooses His people by race, then virtually every "Jew" living in the world is unchosen. They are imposters, fake Jews. That is proven by DNA science.

What a colossal hoax has been perpetrated on Christian Zionists! You who are Christian Zionists have supported Israel all these years and given of your precious time and money. You have worked politically to restore the Jewish nation. By your efforts, the people of Israel have flourished and prospered. And now, you discover that the people whom you have supported all this time are not even blood Jews. They are

Khazars. They have no ties with Abraham, Isaac, or Jacob. They are not the seed. They have no claim to the land. *What do you do now, Christian Zionist?*

Khazars Sought Claim to Palestine

James Dean, intelligence analyst and military author, in his article *(Zionist Design Myth of Jewish Genome to Usurp Palestine*, March 13, 2013) believes the so-called "Jews" from Khazaria, "perpetrated the fraud to support the bogus claim to Palestine which was anchored in their being a separate people." He writes:

> "This distinguished them from all others because they claimed a land title in their blood. They bet the farm on this DNA proof of purchase, a God-given, coded passport to the Palestine. Dr. Elhaik erased the bar code…because it was never in the blood."

"On December 14, 2012, Dr. Eran Elhaik turned almost two generations of Jewish genome research upside down," says Dean. But he went even further. "The young Israeli-American geneticist has charged former researchers with academic fraud. And he has the research to back it up."

According to Dean, Jewish Khazar researchers hoaxed previous results to support their false blood claim to Palestine. But from the time that Israel became a State, he writes, "You had a bunch of atheist, communist Jews shoot their way into the Land with the sole moral cover that, God gave it to us only."

But Dean continues, Dr. Elhaik, in an interview with *Haaretz*, has found that "Israel's groups of Jews in the world today do not share a common Genetic origin…the genome of

Jews is a mosaic of ancient peoples and its origin is largely Khazars."

"The Israel connection is such a tiny part of their (the Jews') genome that it cancels out their DNA claim to the Land," says Dean.

"Is this not poetic justice from Dr. Elhaik," Dean points out, "that he brings us scientific proof of there being no biblical Jewish people as such as they have presented themselves? And does this not make a fraud of the historical anti-Semitic smear, by a people who aren't even Semites?"

Jamai Kani agrees. In an article entitled, "The Myth of the Jewish People" (*Gulf Daily News*, Feb. 23, 2013), he writes, "The notion of the Jewish people as a race, rather than a religion of various races, is without foundation."

"The results of a recently published study by Israeli-American geneticist Dr. Eran Elhaik at Johns Hopkins Medical University have scientifically validated the Khazar hypothesis."

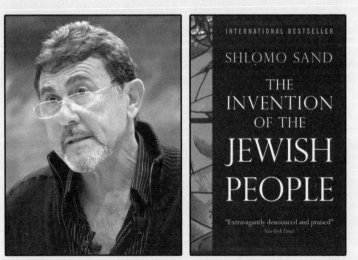

Dr. Shlomo Sand's book, *The Invention of the Jewish People*, in 2007 was a *New York Times* bestseller.

Dr. Shlomo Sand, of the University of Tel Aviv, whose seminal book, *The Invention of the Jewish People* (2007), went to the top of the bestseller lists in Israel and the U.S., warned that the Jewish myth would soon be exposed. The scholarly volume by Sand presents a plethora of historical and archaeological evidence demonstrating that the Jews are not the seed of Abraham. Instead, the Jews today are Khazars.

Khazars Use Trickery, Deception, Murder to Obtain the Land

The racist nature of this land theft is indicated by these statements made by top Jewish Khazar leaders, in regard to their use of trickery, deception, and murder to obtain the land by terror and by ethnic cleansing.

- "Both the process of expropriation and removal of the poor (Palestinians) must be carried out discreetly and circumspectly." (Theodor Herzl, founder of International Zionism, in *The Complete Diaries*, Chapter I, p. 88.)

- "The Palestinian refugees will...simply crumble. Some of them will persist, but the majority will be a human heap, the scum of the earth, and will sink into the lowest levels of the Arab world," (Near East Department of the Israeli government, 1948).

- "There is no other way than to transfer the Arabs from here to the neighboring countries, to transfer all of them; not one village, not one tribe, should be left." (Joseph Weitz, the National Fund Administrator for Zionist colonization from *My*

Diary and Letters to the Children, 1967, Chapter 3, p. 293)

• "The only good Arab is a dead Arab...When we have settled the land, all the Arabs will be able to do about it will be to scurry around like drugged cockroaches in a bottle." (Rafael Eitan, Likud leader of the Tsomet faction (1981) in Noam Chomsky, *Fateful Triangle*, pp 129,130)

• "It is forbidden to be merciful to them, you must with relish—annihilate them. Evil ones, damnable ones. May the Holy Name visit retribution on the Arabs' heads, and cause their seed to be lost, and annihilate them, and cause them to be vanquished and cause them to be cast from the world." (Rabbi Ovadia Yosef, founder and spiritual leader of the Shas party, *Ma'ariv*, April 9, 2001)

• "They (the Palestinians) won't be able to face the war with us, which will include withholding food from Arab cities, preventing education, terminating electric power, and more. They won't be able to exist." (Benzion Netanyahu, father of Prime Minister Benjamin Netanyahu, *Wikipedia*)

Jamai Kani notes that Christians fell hook, line and sinker for the concocted racial tales of the Khazar "Jews." It seemed to fit in with their conceptions, found in the Old Testament, of Jewish superiority. Christians must, he said, now acknowledge that DNA science has exposed their illusions.

"Founded on a melange of myths and

manufactured historical tales, Israel has failed the archaeological test of time and is now exposed by DNA science."

Certainly the Khazars have greatly benefited—and continue to benefit—from these racial myths. Claiming to be true descendants of Abraham, they have cleverly manipulated and used the power of Christian Zionism to forcibly remove the Palestinians from the land. "We are simply obeying God," they repeat over and over.

Christian Zionists not only believed the Khazars but insisted the U.S. government give them all possible support. How could they refuse? They believed they were doing God's work, by insuring that the land promised to the descendants and seed of Abraham became their possession.

The Palestinians May Have More Israelite Blood

What is fascinating is that both Dr. Ariella Oppenheim and Dr. Elhaik, in their DNA research, discovered that a number of Palestinian Moslems—supposedly Gentiles—have at least some connection genetically to the ancient Israelites. Some even have the chromosome which indicates they are ancient "Cohens." The Cohens were the Jews who in olden days attended the Synagogue and temple.

Dr. Ariella Oppenheim in her DNA study, states: "We find that Arabs also carry this (Cohen) chromosome."

Oppenheim, from Hebrew University and the Hadassah Medical School, found that their DNA documents that *both* the Palestinians and the Jews originate from the Kurds of Iraq and Turkey. Thus, they are Khazars and not descendants of Abraham.

Genetic studies, moreover, show that, "as many as 90 percent of the Palestinians have close genetic ties to Jews."

BY MARK ELLIS | SEPTEMBER 16, 2011 · 11:07 PM

↓ Jump to Comments

Many surprised by genetic and cultural links between Palestinians and Jews

Chromosome for the Cohen, "priestly" line shows up in Palestinians

By Mark Ellis

In some of the dry and dusty Palestinian and Bedouin villages they still circumcise their boys after the seventh day. Hidden away in some Palestinian homes are Jewish mezuzahs and tefillin. Some older residents can recall lighting candles on the Sabbath.

Israeli and Palestinian boys

"Many of the Palestinians know it, but it's not politically correct to acknowledge this publicly among Muslims," says Steve Hagerman, fou[...] Outreach. "There are two houses of Israel in the Holy La[...] West and primarily secular or Jewish and the other aligne[...] primarily Islam."

Dr. Ariella Oppenheim's genetics research found the "Cohen" chromosome Y in both Palestinians and Jews.

(*beliefnet.com/news/2011/09/*Jews-Palestinians Have Close Genetic Ties).

Is the Israel-Palestinian conflict much like the U. S. War Between the States, simply a case of brother fighting brother? Are the Jews who actually have some Israelite chromosomes in their DNA in opposition to the Palestinians that have the same Israelite DNA?

After the Oppenheim DNA findings were published in 2001, the editor of the largest daily newspaper in Palestine, a Moslem, challenged the corresponding editor of the largest daily Israel paper, a supposed Jew, to a *"DNA Duel."* He said, *"I have more Israelite blood coursing through my veins than you do!"* The Israeli turned down the challenge and refused to test his blood for DNA. *"No thanks,"* he answered.

Have Christian Zionists long promoted the wrong people, mistakenly believing the Khazars to be blood Jews? Have these imposters (Khazars) used the Christian support to go out and assault and discriminate against people in Israel who actually are more "Jewish" than are they? Bluntly stated—are today's "Jews," in Israel, according to their DNA non-Israelite Khazars? Are they fighting to obtain the land from those, the native-born Palestinians, who possess more Israelite DNA than do they?

How to Make Amends

What do Christian Zionists need to do to put things right? If they are correct that only Abraham's seed has the right to the land, God cannot be pleased that non-Israelites, having no blood link to Abraham, have been given title to the land of Israel. Should Christians now reverse themselves, supporting policies that *dispossess* the Khazar Jews of the land they have grabbed illegally?

DNA science is easy to reproduce. For less than $50 per person, we could take DNA samples from every citizen in Israel and Palestine. Only those proven to be true Jews (perhaps 1 to 2 percent) would be allowed to stay. The Khazars and others would be told, *"You are not of Abraham. You must go. God has given this land only to the seed of Abraham."*

After all, every one of Israel's leaders, their Prime Ministers, has evidently been a false Jew, a Khazar. From the

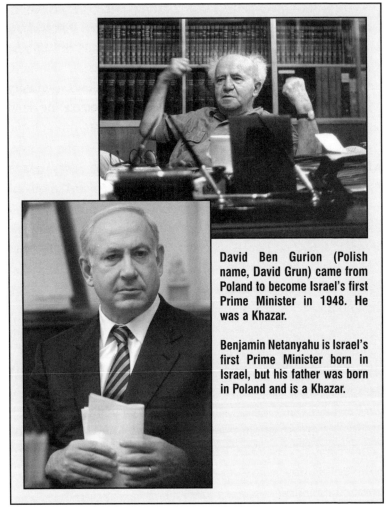

David Ben Gurion (Polish name, David Grun) came from Poland to become Israel's first Prime Minister in 1948. He was a Khazar.

Benjamin Netanyahu is Israel's first Prime Minister born in Israel, but his father was born in Poland and is a Khazar.

days of the first Prime Minister, David Ben Gurion (real name: *David Grun*), all except Benjamin Netanyahu came from Poland. Prime Minister Shimon Peres, also a Pole, is really named Szymon Perski. Meanwhile, Benjamin Netanyahu, the only one born in Israel, has a father who is also from Poland.

Even the Soviet Union's Vladimir Lenin, was a Khazar Jew. His real name was *Vladimir Ulyanov*. The second in command in the Kremlin during the early Communist era was Leon Trotsky (real Jewish Khazar name, *Lev Bronstein*). Karl Marx, too, was of Khazar Jewish origins. So Communism was almost exclusively a Khazar Jewish concoction.

It should be noted that almost all the Jews (actually *Khazars*) who came to Israel in 1948 and seized the land belonging to the Palestinians were, indeed, virulent Communists. Ninety-eight percent of their leadership was from Poland, where the Khazars had settled, beginning in the 10th century. In Tel Aviv, in 1948, they called themselves "Little Poland."

The End Result

If DNA were used to judge who gets the land of Israel and who inhabit it, it is estimated that almost all of the current inhabitants would be Palestinians. There are probably more Palestinians with some ancient Israelite blood than there are so-called "Jews." This end result would, using the Christian Zionists' own standards, be fair and reasonable. Or, would it?

Should we, in fact, use the criterion of who has the most Israelite DNA to ascertain ownership of the land? It seems to me that Christian Zionists should really examine their thinking. The question to be answered is, what is God's criteria for ownership? Are the Israel of God and the Israel of man two entirely separate and distinct entities?

The DNA is Authoritative

It seems that only through DNA can the authenticity of Abraham's descendants be authoritatively established. Authoritative DNA studies have *already* been accomplished. Now the world knows. The Bible is absolutely correct:

> *I know thy works, and tribulation, and poverty, (but thou art rich) and I know the blasphemy of them*

which say they are Jews, and are not, but are the synagogue of Satan. (Revelation 2:9)

Behold, I will make them of the synagogue of Satan, which say they are Jews, and are not, but do lie; behold, I will make them to come and worship before thy feet, and to know that I have loved thee. (Revelation 3:9)

THREE

New DNA Science Research Confirms...

"Jews" Are Not Descendants of Abraham

"I know the blasphemy of them which say they are Jews, and are not, but are the Synagogue of Satan."

—*Revelation 2:9*

Who should possess the land of Israel? Christian evangelicals say it should be the descendants of Abraham. They point to the Old Testament and claim that God gave this land forever to the descendants of Abraham and that God demands they and they alone own the land.

To the Christian evangelical, this means the Jews. Yes, it is the Jews who own this land, and it is their land forever.

The Jews, then, according to Christian evangelicals, are

the descendants of Abraham, his *seed*.

DNA Science Confounds the Common Wisdom

There is only one problem. And it is a huge one. Science proves those who call themselves "Jews" are not Jews! *DNA science has confounded the Christian evangelicals by proving conclusively that most of the people in the nation of Israel and in World Jewry are not the descendants of Abraham.*

Most all those living today who profess to be "Jews" are *not* of the ancient Israelites, and they are *not* the seed of Abraham. In fact, the new DNA research shows that the Palestinians actually have more Israelite blood than do the "Jews!"

The nation of Israel today is populated with seven and half million *imposters*.

The "Jews" Are Not Jews But Are Khazarians

The newest DNA science finding is from Dr. Eran Elhaik ("a Jew") and associates at the McKusick-Nathans Institute of Genetic Medicine, Johns Hopkins University School of Medicine. In research accepted December 5, 2012 and published by the Oxford University Press on behalf of the Society of Molecular Biology and Evolution, it was found that the *"Khazarian Hypothesis"* is scientifically correct.

What exactly is the "Khazarian Hypothesis?" Simply stated, it holds that the Jewry genome is a mosaic of ancestries which rise primarily out of the Khazars. Jews are Khazars, not Israelites.

The "Jews" of America, Europe, and Israel are descendants not of Father Abraham but of King Bulan and the people of ancient Khazaria. Khazaria was an amalgam of Turkic clans who once lived in the Caucasus (Southern Russia). These Turkic peoples were pagans who converted to Judaism in the eighth century. As converts, they called themselves "Jews," but *none* of their blood comes from Israel.

Later, the "Jews" (Khazars) emigrated, settling in Russia, Hungary, Poland, Germany, and elsewhere in Europe. As "Jews," the Khazars then left the European nations in 1948 and settled the fledgling, new nation of Israel.

The people of Israel are not the seed, nor the ancestors, of Abraham. They call themselves "Jews," but in fact, DNA science shows them to be Khazars. They say they are "Jew," but they are not.

"There are no blood or family connections among the Jews," said Dr. Elhaik in an interview with *Haaretz*, Israel's daily newspaper. "The various groups of Jews in the world today do not share a common genetic origin. Their genome is largely Khazar."

God Did Not Give the Land to the Khazarians

Thus, when Prime Minister Netanyahu says, "God gave this land to *our* Israelite forefathers," he is absolutely wrong. There are *no* Israelite forefathers of today's "Jews." When today's "Jews" say they should possess the land because they are Israelites and are the seed of Abraham, they are mistaken.

The "Jews" are in Israel for one reason and one reason only: Because the United States, in 1948, recognized the nation of "Israel" and has since funded and protected it. *God's Word has nothing to do with it.*

God's Word, the Holy Bible, prophesied that in the last days imposters would erroneously and falsely claim to be "Jews." These imposters would, the Bible told us, persecute their enemies and especially the Christians. But God would have his revenge:

> *"Behold, I will make them of the synagogue of*

GENOME BIOLOGY AND EVOLUTION

ABOUT THIS JOURNAL   CONTACT THIS JOURNAL   CURR

Oxford Journals › Life Sciences › Genome Biology and Evolution › Volume 5, Issue 1 › Pp. 61-74.

The Missing Link of Jewish European Ancestry: Contrasting the Rhineland and the Khazarian Hypotheses

Eran Elhaik[1,2,*]

+ Author Affiliations

⌐ *Corresponding author: E-mail: eelhaik@jhsph.edu.

Accepted December 5, 2012.

Abstract

The question of Jewish ancestry has been the subject of controversy for ove[→]
two centuries and has yet to be resolved. The "Rhineland hypothesis" depicts
Eastern European Jews as a "population isolate" that emerged from a small
group of German Jews who migrated eastward and expanded rapidly.
Alternatively, the "Khazarian hypothesis" suggests that Eastern European
Jews descended from the Khazars, an amalgam of Turkic clans that settled
the Caucasus in the early centuries CE and converted to Judaism in the 8th
century. Mesopotamian and Greco-Roman Jews continuously reinforced the
Judaized empire until the 13th century. Following the collapse of their
empire, the Judeo-K
Jewry is therefore e
far, however, the Kh
as the absence of ge
testing the Khazaria
populations prompte
with the Rhineland h
genetic analyses to
Khazarian hypothesi
of Near Eastern–Cau
consolidating previo
describe a major dif
early presence of Ju
have important impli
genetic diversity in t

Dr. Eran Elhaik, geneticist researcher at Johns Hopkins University School of Medicine, found that today's "Jews" originated from Khazaria and not Israel. They are not the seed of Abraham.

Satan, which say they are Jews, and are not, but do lie; behold, I will make them to come and worship before thy feet, and to know that I have loved thee."
(Revelation 3:9)

Do the "Jews" (Khazars) not do exactly as our God prophesied? Do they not persecute the Palestinians and defile the land, claiming *they* are its original inhabitants? This, even though their *proven* ancestors, the Khazars, never set foot in the Middle East and are *not* the seed of Abraham?

My thanks to Dr. Eran Elhaik of Johns Hopkins University and to his associates. You have performed a valuable service with your DNA research, both to Christianity and to world understanding. Elhaik's research confirms earlier DNA studies, especially the work of Dr. Ariella Oppenheim of Hebrew University, who likewise found, in 2001, that the "Jews" came from the Khazars rather than the Israelites. Dr. Oppenheim even found that some of the Palestinians have the chromosomes proving they are "Cohen," related to the ancient Israelites who worked in the Synagogue and Temple.

Where, and Who, Are the Seed of Abraham?

I ask my evangelical Christian friends: What will you do now? Will you heed what God said, in *Revelation 2* and *3*, about "them which say they are Jews and are not?" Will you accept modern DNA science as legitimate and valuable in proving the truth of God's Word?

Or will you, dear Christian friend, walk right on by, dismissing what both God and science have informed you?

God said that the seed of Abraham would inherit the land. If we believe this, we must—absolutely must—in light of the DNA evidence, ask ourselves: Where, and who are the seed of Abraham?

We know that Netanyahu and the people who now inhabit Israel have no claim to the land. They are interlopers, false pretenders. But there is a true and legitimate Chosen People of God. In fact, the scriptures had it right all along. The answer is found in *Galatians 3:29*. Read it for yourself:

> *"And if ye be Christ's, then are ye Abraham's seed, and heirs according to the promise."*

So, if you belong to Jesus our Lord, you are "Abraham's seed," regardless of your physical race. You are overcomers, and *Revelation 21:7* promises, "He that overcometh shall inherit all things." This is the great secret that every true Christian should know.

God is not a racist. The Great Commission extends to every race and ethnicity. We who love Jesus are His Chosen People, and we have the promise first given to Abraham way back in Genesis.

Know this, and you will forever be greatly blessed. And that, dear friends is the promise given Abraham and his seed.

FOUR

The "Jews" Are Not The Seed of Abraham

How the Racial Hoax of the Jews Was Finally Exposed

The newest DNA scientific studies, showing that almost all the people known today as the Jews of Israel—and, indeed Jews all over the world—are, in fact, of Khazar, *not Israelite* origins, is backed by the earlier work of historians.

These historians found that their scholarly books and reports were immediately attacked by Zionists desperate to maintain the fiction that the Jews could trace their heritage all the way back to Abraham.

The Zionists knew the truth—that they are not a race but a composite of many races. They had to keep up the myth that they were a homogenous race kept together by religion and community interests for 5,000 years. Only in this way could the Zionist Jews claim to be the seed of Abraham. Only as

"Israelites" could the Jews claim possession to land where they and their ancestors had never been.

The Zionists knew, too, that their genocide and ethnic cleansing against the Palestinians was not justified *unless* they, the Jews, had claim to the land. How else could they get the millions of evangelical Christians to support their horrible behavior? If they were suspected of being converts to Judaism and not actually the tribes mentioned in the Bible, it was all over for them. Their Lie would be out—they would be seen for what they are—imposters.

Pulling Off the Hoax

The Zionists Jews were able to pull off their racial hoax for decades, even though historians and anthropologists—many of them Jewish—wrote book after book. In 1899, famous British historian Houston Stewart Chamberlain published *The Foundations of the Nineteenth Century*, which held that the Jews were *not* a race, but instead, were "bastards." (At the time, *bastards* was not a pejorative word)

Yitzhak Schipper, quoted extensively by Jacob Litman's *The Economic Role of Jews in Medieval Poland*, affirmed that the Khazars were the "Jews." In 1867, the great Jewish scholar Abraham Harkavy, in *The Jews and Languages of the Slavs*, spoke of the Jewish Yiddish language coming from the Khazars.

It was, however, a prominent Jew named Arthur Koestler, himself a Zionist Jew, who in 1976 published the book which caused such a sensation. *The Thirteenth Tribe* was a literary bombshell. Koestler's accurate work was meant to be a refutation of Hitler and the Nazis, but it had incredible unintended consequences. He wrote:

"The large majority of surviving Jews in the world

is of Eastern European—thus perhaps mainly of Khazar—origin. If so, this would mean that their (the Jews) ancestors came not from Canaan but from the Caucasus, once believed to be the cradle of the Aryan race, and that genetically they are more closely related to the Hun, Ulgur, and Magyar tribes than to the seed of Abraham, Isaac, and Jacob... The story of the Khazar Empire, as it slowly emerges from the past, begins to look like the most cruel hoax which history has ever perpetrated."

Koestler, who thought he was doing his fellow Jews a service, was unmercifully attacked by other Zionists who felt he had let the cat out of the bag. If they come from the Khazars and are not of Israelite origin, the Jews had no ancestral claim to the land of Israel. They were not the seed of Abraham but of King Bulan and the people of Khazaria.

Arthur Koestler's famous book, *The Thirteenth Tribe* has been vindicated by DNA research.

As Shlomo Sand, history professor at the University of Tel Aviv, explains it in his outstanding, 2007 book, *The Invention of the Jewish People*, "Without the Old Testament in its hand and the exile of the Jewish people in its memory, Israel would have no justification for annexing Arab Jerusalem and establishing settlements in the West Bank, the Gaza Strip, the Golan Heights, and even the Sinai Peninsula."

If they were Khazars, the title, the "Eternal People" did not apply to them. They would be, in fact, another usurping ethnic conglomerate, falsely claiming to be "Jews" and willing to kill to illegally possess the rightful ancestral lands of the Palestinians.

Other books followed, most notably Kevin Brook's 1999, *The Jews of Khazaria*. But these many scholarly books never really became the consensus because of Zionist opposition. As Orwell once wrote, *"Whoever controls history controls the world."*

DNA Science Introduces Stark Reality

Until 1968, that is, when the two British scientists, Watson and

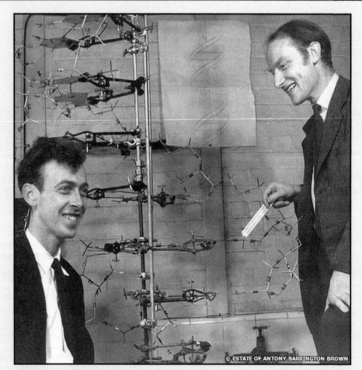

Watson and Crick, were British researchers who, in 1968, discovered the importance of DNA.

Crick, came up with DNA science. Since 1968, DNA has become the principal science used in criminology, both to convict and to exonerate. It has become so popular that "DNA Kits" can be purchased so individuals can have their own blood tested to determine their heritage, down to the last percentile.

Because of DNA science, historians and anthropologists have been able to find missing links and to unravel the mysteries of race and ethnology.

In 2001, Dr. Ariella Oppenheim, of Hebrew University, a biologist, published the first extensive study of DNA and the origin of the Jews. Her research found that virtually all the Jews came from Turkish and Kurd blood. Not only that but Oppenheim suggested that the Palestinians—the very people whom the Jews had been persecuting and ejecting from Israel's land since 1948—might have more Israelite blood than did the Jews. In sum, the vast majority of the Jews were not Jews; some of the Palestinians were. Some of the Palestinians even had a DNA chromosome which established that they were "Cohens"—workers at the ancient Temple and synagogues of the Jews.

The Definitive DNA Study

Now comes the ultimate, definitive DNA study, by Dr. Eran Elhaik and associates at the McKusick-Nathans Institute of Genetic Medicine, Johns Hopkins University School of Medicine. Entitled, *The Missing Link of Jewish European Ancestry: Contrasting the Rhineland and the Khazarian Hypotheses*, and published by the *Oxford Journal* on behalf of the Society for Molecular Biology and Evolution, the study confirms Oppenheim's research and the many scholarly books.

Dr. Elhaik and the prestigious Johns Hopkins University

School of Medicine conclude in their report: *"The Khazarian Hypothesis suggests that Eastern European Jews descended from the Khazars, an amalgam of Turkic clans that settled the Caucasus in the early centuries CE and Converted to Judaism in the eighth century... Following the collapse of their empire, the Judeo-Khazars fled to Eastern Europe. The rise of European Jewry is therefore explained by the contribution of the Judeo-Khazars."*

Who Can Argue With DNA Science?

So DNA science has proven that the findings of many historians and anthropologists is correct. The "Jews" of Israel are not Abraham's descendants but, instead, come from the subjects of King Bulan of Khazaria.

Now everything changes.

FIVE

New Scientific Discoveries Demolish Jewish Supremacy Theory

Impure Blood

"We Jews regard our race as superior to all humanity, and look forward...to its triumph over them."

> — Goldwin Smith (Jew)
> Professor of Modern History,
> Oxford University

I was fascinated by an article I read recently on the internet by a Jewish columnist. It was entitled, *Who Jew?* The columnist was quite proud of his race and bragged on and on endlessly about the achievements throughout history of the Jews, especially in such fields as entertainment, movies, literature, and culture. He went on to name many such Jews, celebrities, names like Rodney Dangerfield, Charlie Chaplin, Sharon Stone, and Barbra Streisand.

51

I was, of course, familiar with the repeated, boastful, arrogant claims of Jews. But, the whole thing is getting a little tiring. I am growing weary of reading and hearing what, to me, are so many examples of racist braggadocio on the part of Jews. It's one thing to be proud of who you are, of your race. It's quite another to stake the outrageous claim that your DNA, your flesh, your blood makes you God's Chosen, the superior race, destined to rule over the stupid, inferior goyim (cattle, e.g. Gentile races).

Jews Boast of Racial Supremacy

Consider these prideful statements attributed to Jews:

"One million Arabs aren't worth a Jewish fingernail."
—Rabbi Yaacov Perrin
The New York Times,
Feb. 28, 1994, p.1

"There is a huge gap between us and our enemies. They do not belong to our continent, our world, but actually belong to a different galaxy."
— Moshe Katsave,
Israeli President
The Jerusalem Post,
May 10, 2001

"The Palestinians are beasts walking on two legs."
— Menachem Begin,
Prime Minister of Israel
New Statesman,
June 25, 1982

"Our race will take its rightful place in the world, with every Jew a king and every Gentile a slave."
— Rabbi Emmanuel Rabbinovich
Common Sense,
January 12, 1952

Jewish revolutionary Adam Weishaupt, founder of the Order of the Illuminati (1776), and Soviet Communist Jews Lenin and Trotsky would no doubt be proud of such obviously ethnocentric, pro-Zionist sentiments. And, it seems to me many Christian evangelicals, dyed-in-the-wool Judaizers as they are, might also applaud. After all, the Judaizers firmly believe that God favors the Jews. They teach that God has chosen them forever as His own people, and that he gave the Jews the land forever.

If, therefore, the Jews have grabbed and stolen the land, murdering the poor Palestinians whose ancestors have lived on it for centuries and centuries up to now, then, so be it. Thievery and murder in pursuit of promoting the financial and other interests of the superior Jewish race can't be bad, can it? No, certainly not! Just serving God, right?

A Terrible Dilemma Raises its Ugly Head

However, surprisingly, a terrible, terrible dilemma has surfaced. Yes, a horrible problem has arisen. If it is true that the Jews are "God's Chosen," His superior blood race; and if it is true that they, and only they, have been given the land forever by an exclusive covenant with God, then—ok. But...but...but...

HOW DO WE KNOW WHO THE REAL JEWS ARE?

Put more succinctly and more to the point:

IS THERE, IN FACT, A SINGLE REAL JEW LEFT ON THE FACE OF PLANET EARTH?

The new scientific DNA research and historical discoveries—which only now are beginning to be understood by the average John Q. Citizen—have horrified high-level Jews. Genetic specialists at Johns Hopkins University, Oxford University in England, at Harvard University in Boston, Hebrew University in Israel, the University of Arizona, and other distinguished institutions, using up-to-date DNA testing methods and databases, have come to an astonishing conclusion: *Nowhere on earth is there anyone who truly is a pure Jew!*

The new DNA research came from Dr. Ariella Oppenheim, a Jewish professor of genetics at Hebrew University in Israel, and five research colleagues. Their findings, reported in the *American Journal of Human Genetics* (November 2001), that Jews are closely related in DNA to Iraqis, Kurds, Turks, and Armenians. Meanwhile, Sephardic (Middle East Jews) differ from European Jews, many of whom were found to be of Khazar (Turkic) stock.

That was 2001. Then, in late 2012, Dr. Eran Elhaik, Israeli-born genetics researcher out of John Hopkins Medical University in Baltimore, Maryland published his colossal findings in an article, *The Missing Link of Jewish European Ancestry: Contrasting the Rhineland and the Khazarian Hypotheses*. Published in the authoritative journal, *Genome Biology and Evolution* of Oxford University Press, the scholars who peer-reviewed the article described it as more profound and accurate than all the previous studies on the ancestry of the Jewish study.

What was Dr. Elhaik's remarkable finding? He found that the genetics (DNA) material of today's Jews are, in fact, not related in any way to that of the ancient Israelites. Instead, as historians and archeologists have long maintained, today's "Jews" are descendants of the Caucasian nation known as Khazaria. Jews are Khazarians, not the seed of Abraham, Isaac, and Jacob.

Do Palestinians Have More Israelite Blood?

What's more, there is no doubt about it, the new DNA research proves that the Arabs and Palestinians—yes, the foes of today's "Jews"—have as much or even more ancient Israelite blood in their bodies as do the people in Israel and Europe who call themselves "Jews" and are identified as "Jews."

In other words, a typical Palestinian, Syrian, Kurd, or Iraqi named Ahmed, Mohammed, or Hussein may well be more of an Israelite than a man or woman today living in Israel or America who claims to be "Jew" and goes by the name, say, of Weinstein, Goldberg, Greenspan, Rubin, Stein, Rosenberg, Foxman, Sharon, or Netanyahu!

As *The New York Times* reported, "According to a new scientific study, Jews are the genetic brothers of Palestinians, Syrians, and Lebanese, and they all share a common genetic lineage."

The Proceedings of the National Academy of Sciences (June 6, 2000) found that Jewish men—or at least, men who identified themselves as "Jew"—share a common set of genetic signatures with non-Jews (Arabs) from the Mid-East region." In effect, the people we call Arabs and Jews are actually brothers in genetic makeup.

The Secret is Out!

Stuart Wilde, popular speaker and writer, suggests the secret is out; thanks to findings of the new scientific DNA research, favored treatment for people just because they say they are Jews is breaking down...

"Of course, the Jews could give up their racism and their 'chosen people' bigotry and make peace with humanity. They claim to have special blood, but modern DNA makes a mockery of that. Middle Eastern Jews have the same DNA as the Palestinian people, who they consider goyim (cattle), sub-human. European Jews have European DNA. It's tragic how foolish the ego can be, utterly sad, pathetic in a way."

Naturally, the Jews who comprise the Illuminati elite are extremely alarmed over these new scientific revelations. They are concerned about the implications. Up to now, all one has had to do to prove Jewish ancestry, according to Jewish law, was to produce some man-made document or other "evidence" showing one's "Jewish heritage" on the matriarchal side of the bloodline. But, horror of horrors, the biological scientists, in researching the matriarchal DNA lineage, have discovered *there is absolutely no linkage at all between modern-day, so-called "Jews" and the DNA of ancient Israelites.* Oh my!

The late Christopher Hitchens, the well-known political commentator and Jewish author, did an article in *Forward*, the popular Jewish publication regularly read by tens of thousands of American Jews. Hitchens declared that the new DNA studies offer a dramatic and different future for those who say they are Jews. He jokingly quipped that Jews today are evidently no longer full Semites, so they must be "Semi-Semites."

Hitchens also sagely writes: "According to the law of Moses, the Law of Return, Israel's civil code and the Nuremburg Laws, I am a Jew." But, he continues, "Recent advances in DNA testing have either simplified or complicated the claims of holy books and founding texts."

"Ethnic Purity is a Fantasy"

Admitting that "ethnic purity is a fantasy," Hitchens goes on to note the results of a match-up between the genetic database of the Kohanim—Jewish men named Cohen whose Jewish ancestry is supposedly the strongest and best-attested—and that of a "lost Jewish tribe," the Lemba of Africa, in the country of Namibia. The black Africans have long claimed to be Israelites, but whiter Jews typically laughed and sneered.

Guess what? Scientists now say the blacks of the Lemba tribe were right all along:

> "A riveting essay in the (Jewish publication) Commentary described the results...The genetic fit was amazingly close. So it is with other groups..."

"How long," asked Hitchens, "before we can codify Khazar (Mongul/Turk) DNA and find out if Koestler was right or if the Ashkenazim (European Jews) have any genetic claim to Gaza?"

Too bad Hitchens died in 2011, only a year before Dr. Eran Elhaik's monumental study at John Hopkins University in Baltimore, Maryland was published confirming that the Ashkenazi Jews have no genetic claim to Gaza and Palestine.

Jews Who Are Africans and Indians

Hitchens did hit on the problem, the big, big problem for the Israeli and Jewish elite who are striving to maintain the fiction of racial, or ethnic, purity. Already, the scientists had discovered that some black Africans are, indeed, Jews, but also that a community of people in the nation of India are Jewish-related according to their DNA. They look like Indians, of course, but they have as much "Jewish" DNA as do "Jewish people living in Israel." They even have *more* Jewish blood (DNA) than do many European Jews.

In fact, in one recent scientific study of European Jews it was found that almost 88 percent of these people have no Jewish DNA stock whatsoever!

Say what? Yep, that's right. It turns out that the Jews are not of Israelite origin at all. They are of Khazar origin. Before, this was all theory. Now it is fact. Many Jews are Khazars and neither they nor their ancestors were Israelites. They are not related genetically to the ancient Israelites. So the question arises: Do those people who say they are Jews and are not deserve the land? Obviously, they are not the physical seed of Abraham. Their DNA proves that. Does the eternal covenant apply to them? Should we throw these racial imposters out?

"Avoid Foolish Questions and Genealogies"

It appears that the Holy Bible also has had it right all along. The scriptures wisely advise us to discard our foolish notions about race and accept the truism that God is no respecter of persons. The Apostle Paul wrote: *"Neither give heed to fables and endless genealogies." (1 Timothy 1:4)*

Then, to emphasize the point, he stated: *"But avoid foolish questions, and genealogies, and contentions... for they are unprofitable and vain." (Titus 3:9)*

Wow! So, figuring out genealogies and attempting to exalt a people based on their racial origins is foolish, unprofitable, and vain. But clearly, the Judaizers care not a whit what the Bible says. They are obsessed with racial supremacy fantasies and with pursuing endless genealogies.

Who Gets the Land?

Who, then, gets the land? To be fair, should we not administer a DNA test to every Arab and Jew living in the world and find out who has the most ancient Israelite DNA? Why not? Let's find out who really is a Jew. Who really are the ones, if any, whose father was Abraham? If Netanyahu, the Prime Minister of Israel isn't really a Jew, but the Palestinian Authority's President has more ancient Israelite DNA, then, by all means, lets appoint the Palestinian as the new and authentic Prime Minister of Israel. Or maybe we should give that post to a black man from the Lemba tribe in Africa. In fact, maybe a brown skinned Hindu from India deserves to be Prime Minister. Maybe the India "Jews" own the land as *their* eternal possession.

After all, it is a matter of race isn't it? The Jewish race. If, however, it were a matter of *religion*, of who is a Jew based on allegiance to the religion of Judaism, then the late actor Sammy Davis, Jr. a converted Jew, or the late, blonde, bombshell actress Marilyn Monroe, yet another converted Jew, could have legitimately been heirs to the Promise. As Jews by religious preference, were Davis and Monroe not "God's Chosen?" Maybe their heirs living today deserve the land.

Indeed, today's vulgar porno singers Madonna and Britney Spears, and foul-mouthed comedians Roseanne Barr and Whoopi Goldberg, by virtue of their study of the Jewish Cabala, are Jews and own the land! If devotion to the Jewish religion is what counts, these reprobates are truly of the seed of Abraham!

Whatever is the case, it is a fact that the Judaizer Christians are beginning to look spectacularly stupid—and pitifully racist and bigoted to boot! Graham, Lindsey, Hagee and the others apparently tout the whiter Jews as the real Jews. But why should only white men get the land? What about black and brown Jews. Hindu Jews, Buddhist Jews?

Scientists confirm that nowhere on earth is there a pure

Jew. Scientifically, there is no such thing biologically as the "Jewish race." They are all Heinz 57, multiple racial flavors like Baskin-Robbins ice cream. So which "Jews" will the Judaizers bestow the rewards on?

Anyone Can Be A Jew

As one wry internet writer observes, anyone can say, "I'm a Jew," and no-one can prove them right or wrong:

> "Yes they can be Jews. You could have a bunch of garbage collectors who decide to call themselves Jews. A political group can identify itself as Jewish, or any other kind of group can. Maybe Africans or Greeks or Chinese—they can say it too, and they might be right scientifically.
>
> There is nothing stopping anyone from calling themselves Jews. They can even say, 'I'm a descendant of the Israelites. I deserve this land, God gave it to me.'
>
> And all the so-called Jews living in Israel have no more right to the land than do the newcomers who say they are the real Jews. Which ones will the Christians give the land to? Which are the real and which are the counterfeits? Who gets the gold?"

It Pays to Claim You are a Jew...Or Does It?

Who Jew? the man asked in his article. Well, no-one, comes the scientific answer. Still, certain men continue to self-identify as Jews. Why? Could greed be the answer? There's no benefit in being an Italian, a Belgian, a Mexican, or an Indian. But there are tremendous advantages to being a Jew. It pays to be a Jew! You get to be special and chosen, and you get someone else's land. And if they complain, well, just kill them. As Rabbi Yaacov Perrin says, a million of them aren't worth a single Jew's fingernail!

But, on the other hand, it will someday, perhaps very soon, be very dangerous to be a "Jew," especially if you're not a real Jew (And scientifically, no-one is). You see, God doesn't much appreciate racists, liars, people who steal land, people who make themselves out to be something they are not, and especially people who blaspheme the name of Jesus falsely claiming He was not the Son of God.

So, watch out, you who say you are Jews and are not, but do lie. In your racial fantasies, you may imagine that, someday, all the Gentiles of earth shall be your slaves. But, you are going to be proven dead wrong.

Racially, there are no real Jews left on earth. God knows the people who are racial imposters. He knows of their excess, arrogant pride and of their tragic hatred of mankind. God rejects their racism, he has no use for their foolish genealogies, and unless they repent, they are in deep, dire trouble:

> *"I know the blasphemy of them which say they are Jews, and are not, but are the synagogue of Satan... He that hath an ear, let him hear what the Spirit saith unto the churches..." (Revelation 2:9,11)*

SIX

Race and Khazaria

"God gave the title to this land (Israel) to the
Jews over 5,000 years ago. It is their land."
— Former Governor Mike Huckabee
The Mike Huckabee Show
(Fox News, 2012)

"Our findings support the Khazarian
Hypothesis. The Jews came from ancient
Khazarian ancestry."
— Dr. Eran Elhaik
Johns Hopkins Medical University
The Nathan Musick School of
Genetic Sciences
(December 2012)

Christian Zionists always make note of what
they believe to be the purity of the Jewish race.
It is this racial quality, they say, which makes
the Jews a unique and peculiar people. "Only the Jews have
been preserved pure by God for thousands of years," they say

with confidence. The Christian Zionists believe that the Jews are a distinct and separate race, peculiar to all others, and have remained distinct over the centuries since Abraham. Their religious theories hold that the Jews are God's Chosen People. It is they alone, of all the races, that God loves the most, has preserved, and will continue to keep pure forever.

DNA science has to be a huge blow to the confidence of Christian Zionists. Yet, some Jews themselves have been leery of ascribing purity to their race. Rabbi Harold M. Schulweiss states that Judaism is *not* a biological entity, racial or ethnic. "The Jew is not a matter of genes and chromosomes... Judaism is not rooted in race or clan or in a genetic matter but is a religious tradition of choice." (www.khazaria.com/genetics/abstracts.html)

Rabbi Rami Shapiro writes: "There is only one response to 'Who is a Jew?' that works. A Jew is one who takes Judaism seriously."

Rabbi Jonathan Sacks is one of Jewry's most famous rabbis. In his book, *Future Tense: Jews, Judaism, and Israel in the Twenty-First Century*, he concedes that Arthur Koestler's theory of Khazar origins has much to offer. "Judaism is not an ethnicity and Jews are not an ethnic group," Sacks writes. "Go to the Western Wall in Jerusalem and you will see Jews of every color and culture under the sun."

But the voices of these Jews is drowned out by the Jews who insist they are unique and special, a separate people whom God bequeathed the land to some 5,000 years ago. They are, they contend, Abraham's seed, God's Chosen People, supra-humans. Their Talmud and Kabbalah reinforce this view, stating that the Jewish race is destined to rule planet earth. Thus, the rabbinical Jews are preparing for this day and continue to act as superior human beings, even as "gods" on earth.

"Jews" Worry They Will Lose Their Special Status

Shlomo Sand of the University of Tel Aviv, in *The Invention of the Jewish People*, says that the Jews have long feared "any element that might challenge the myth" of Judaic Abrahamic origins. "Even nationalists who were confirmed atheists resorted to religious symbols in their self-definition, while respected clergymen accepted the principle of 'blood' as a boundary marker." He writes:

> "Zionism adopted the most exclusionary and conceited aspect of the Jewish religious tradition... The ancient ideal of an elect, holy, monotheistic congregation was reinterpreted in an isolationist, secular plan of action. Zionism from its inception was an ethnocentric nationalist movement that firmly enclosed the historical people of its own invention... At the same time any withdrawal from the people was depicted as an unforgivable offense, and assimilation as a catastrophe, an existential danger to be averted at all costs."

After 1948, the Jews became paranoid, says Sand, so anxious were they that unless they were of Abraham, the nation of Israel would be delegitimized. The world, particularly the United States, would deny their right to exist. If they were not Israelites, they reasoned, they had no claim to Israel as a nation.

Sand says that, "biology was conscripted to reinforce the (false) notion of the 'ancient Jewish nation.'" Now, with the advent of DNA science, the Jews are exposed. They no longer can claim to be descendants of Abraham. The Jews are not a blood race that has retained its purity all these generations. The very thing that the Jews used to enforce the concept of nationhood, biology, is being used to dismantle their long built wall of racial separation. The Jews are not who they think they are. They are no different than any other peoples.

Time to Rejoin the Human Race

Sand believes it is time for the Jews to rejoin the human race, to jettison their presumed exclusivity. It is a long-time coming, he notes, and he tells the story of none other than Theodor Herzl, the founder of the Zionist movement, to illustrate his point. Theodor Herzl could not decide if the Jews arose from one source, that is, from Abraham:

> "One evening in London, Herzl dined with the Anglo-Jewish author Israel Zangwill, who would later join the Zionist movement. In his personal diary that day, the handsome leader expressed dismay that the writer, who was famously ugly, thought that they shared the same origin. 'He obsesses about the racial aspect, which I cannot accept. It's enough for me to look at myself and at him. I say only this: We are a historical entity, a nation made up of different anthropological elements. That will suffice for the Jewish state. No nation has racial uniformity.'"

As a result of the Jews' insistence that their "biological uniqueness" as descendants of Abraham and as heirs to the promise of Land given Israel by God, they have been frightened over historical and archeological findings concerning Khazaria. From the 1930s to the 1960s, Sand writes, "hardly anything was published about the Khazars, and those few publications were mostly devoted to their repudiation and denigration."

The Jews, being Khazars, refused knowledge of their own nation and insisted they were *not* Khazars!

Khazaria, Home of the "Jews"

The idea that the Jews came from Khazaria and had no ethnic connection to ancient Israel is for the Khazar Jews extremely menacing. This tendency to close their ears and deny their Khazarian roots continues to this day. No doubt, the fear by Jews of being exposed as interlopers on the Land of Israel is well-founded.

Theodor Herzl, called the "Founder of Israel," believed there was no pure Jewish race.

Regardless of the Jews' reluctance to admit their Khazar roots, a number of scholars and researchers have brought forth their findings about the Khazar nation and its link to today's Jews. The Jew, Abraham Pollok, is one such scholar. His *Khazaria: The History of a Jewish Kingdom in Europe*, in 1951, reported that, "The great bulk of Eastern European Jewry originated in the territories of the Khazar empire," an empire of Turks and Mongolians.

Another researcher of note was Kevin Brook, whose *The Jews of Khazaria*, was first published in 1999 and is now in a second edition. The website khazaria.com says this about Brook's volume:

The Jews of Khazaria recounts the eventful history of the Turkic kingdom of Khazaria, which was located in eastern Europe and flourished as an independent state from about 650 to 1016. As a major world power, Khazaria enjoyed diplomatic and trade relations with many peoples and nations (including the Byzantines, Alans, Magyars, and Slavs) and changed the course of medieval history in many ways.

Did you know that if not for the Khazars, much of eastern Europe would have been overrun by the Arabs and become Islamic? In the same way as Charles Martel and his Franks stopped the advance of Muslims at the Battle of Poitiers in the West, the Khazars blunted the northward advance of the Arabs that was surging across the Caucasus in the 8th century.

The Khazar people belonged to a grouping of Turks who wrote in a runic script that originated in Mongolia. The royalty of the Khazar kingdom was descended from the Ashina Turkic dynasty. In the ninth century, the Khazarian royalty and nobility as well as a significant portion of the Khazarian Turkic population embraced the Jewish religion. After their conversion, the Khazars were ruled by a succession of Jewish kings and began to adopt the hallmarks of Jewish civilization, including the Torah and Talmud, the Hebrew script, and the observance of Jewish holidays.

This volume traces the development of the Khazars from their early beginnings as a tribe to the decline and fall of their kingdom. It demonstrates that Khazaria had manufacturing industries, trade routes, an organized judicial system, and a diverse population. It also examines the many migrations of the Khazar people into Hungary, Ukraine, and other areas of Europe and their subsequent assimilation, providing the most comprehensive treatment of this complex issue to date. The final chapter enumerates the Jewish communities of eastern Europe which sprung up...

In 2008, Russian archaeologist Dmitry Vasilyev unearthed Itil, the long lost capital of the Kingdom of Khazaria. New DNA science proves that today's "Jews" come from Khazaria and are not the seed of Abraham.

However, the books by Pollok and Brook were exceptions and Sand notes that the absence of historical and archeological research on Jews in Khazaria is telling. The fact is that Jewish scholars and researchers have been fearful of their fellow Jews and refrained from publishing their works.

Arthur Koestler's The Thirteenth Tribe

Arthur Koestler, a well-known Jewish writer, really felt the heat from Jews in 1976 when he published what became a sensational book about Khazar and the Jews. His book, *The Thirteenth Tribe*, appeared in Hebrew and English but even though it made *The New York Times Bestsellers List*, Jewish bookshops banned it.

One can understand why the Jewish nation was afraid of Koestler's explosive research when you read the book. It is a comprehensive survey of Khazarian history, and in it Koestler shows how that history dovetails with that of the Jews. Koestler writes:

"The large majority of surviving Jews in the world is of Eastern European—and thus perhaps mainly of Khazar—origin. If so, this would mean that their ancestors came not from Jordan but from the Volga, not from Canaan but from the Caucasus, once believed to be the cradle of the Aryan race; and that genetically they are more closely related to the Hun, Uigur and Magyar tribes than to the seed of Abraham, Isaac and Jacob. Should this turn out to be the case, then the term "anti-Semitism" would become void of meaning, based on a misapprehension shared by both the killers and their victims. The story of the Khazar Empire, as it slowly emerges from the

past, begins to look like the most cruel hoax
which history has ever perpetrated."

Koestler was a Zionist Jew, and he did not believe his well-researched book would damage the ability of the Jews—who he knew from his research to be of Khazar Turk-Mongol stock—to continue in their domination of the nation of Israel. He was incorrect in this regard. DNA science has validated Koestler's work, and now the Jewish nation stands naked before the whole world, a world that increasingly views the nation of Israel as an aberration in history, a prime example of a brutal people manipulating public opinion and using violence and lies to grab hold of land that never was theirs to have.

The Khazars: Skull Caps, Magog, and the Six-Pointed Star

In Koestler's book, we discover that the Khazars are expert at money and finance management. We find that they joined their brand of Judaism with their pagan customs. The adoption of the skullcap *(yarmulke)* by the Jews came from the Khazars in Poland as did the use in that nation for other garb, particularly the fox-fur cap, the *shtreimel*. The Khazars' passion for gefilte fish is mentioned, too.

The Khazars, Koestler explains, claimed to be descendants of *Magog*, and so we have a link with the Bible's Gog and Magog reference.

Other sources tell of the Khazars' adoption of the six-pointed star as their national symbol and shield.

Neturei Karta, a group of Jews opposed to Zionism, in their newsletter reported on this use by the Khazars of the six-pointed star, which the Jews today mistakenly call the "Jewish Star of David:"

"Engravings resembling the Jewish Star of David

were unearthed at two Khazar sites, one along the Donets River in eastern Ukraine and the other along the Don River in southern Russia. This one is a circular metal disc, interpreted by Professor Bozena Werbart of Umea University as Jewish but seen by others as shamanistic or pagan. The circular nature of the disc may represent the sun, and the 6 points represent rays of the sun. Scholars lean towards assigning the disc to Tengri shamanism due to the fact that there are known examples of Khazarian sun discs with 5 or 7 points, rather than consistently 6. Some of the Jewish-Turkic graves at Chelarevo in what used to be Hungary contain engravings of the Star and belong to Khazar Kabar migrants."

King Bulan's Luxurious Lifestyle

As to why the Kagan (King) of Khazaria in the 8th century chose Judaism to be the official religion of his great country,

Khazaria was often in conflict with the Mongols. Note the six-pointed star on the Khazarian shield.

Koestler explains that King Bulan no longer wanted to reign over a primitive pagan nation. He had Christianity, Islam, and Judaism as his three choices. He chose Judaism. That he selected Judaism may be because he saw in that religion similarities to his own opulent lifestyle. An ancient manuscript by one Ibn Fadlan speaks of the King's supreme majesty and power, of his magnificent palace, his harem, and the "Paradise" he expected to go to upon his death. It sounds as if he is speaking about the life and times of King Solomon:

> "Concerning the King of the Khazars, whose title is Kagan, he appears in public only once every four months. They call him the Great Kagan. His deputy is called Kagan Bek; he is the one who commands and supplies the armies, manages the affairs of state, appears in public and leads in war. The neighbouring kings obey his orders. He enters every day into the presence of the Great Kagan, with deference and modesty, barefooted, carrying a stick of wood in his hand. He makes obeisance, lights the stick, and when it has burned down, he sits down on the throne on the King's right. Next to him in rank is a man called the K-nd-r Kagan, and next to that one, the Jawshyghr Kagan.

> "It is the custom of the Great Kagan not to have social intercourse with people, and not to talk with them, and to admit nobody to his presence except those we have mentioned. The power to bind or release, to mete out punishment, and to govern the country belongs to his deputy, the Kagan Bek.

"It is a further custom of the Great Kagan that when he dies a great building is built for him, containing twenty chambers, and in each chamber a grave is dug for him. Stones are broken until they become like powder, which is spread over the floor and covered with pitch. Beneath the building flows a river, and this river is large and rapid. They divert the river water over the grave and they say that this is done so that no devil, no man, no worm and no creeping creatures can get at him. After he has been buried, those who buried him are decapitated, so that nobody may know in which of the chambers is his grave. The grave is called "Paradise" and they have a saying: 'He has entered Paradise.' All the chambers are spread with silk brocade interwoven with threads of gold.

"It is the custom of the King of the Khazars to have twenty-five wives; each of the wives is the daughter of a king who owes him allegiance. He takes them by consent or by force. He has sixty girls for concubines, each of them of exquisite beauty."

The Jews Came from Khazaria

Arthur Koestler's *The Thirteenth Tribe*, is, in fact, the story of the Jews before they were Jews—when they were Khazars. And he notes that the cumulative evidence is that the Khazar contribution to the genetic makeup of today's world Jewry is substantial, if not dominant, an assertion borne out by modern DNA science:

"The numerical ration of the Khazar to the Semitic and other contributions is impossible to establish. But the cumulative evidence makes one inclined to agree with the consensus of Polish historians that 'in earlier times the main bulk originated from the Khazar country;' and that, accordingly, the Khazar contribution to the genetic make-up of the Jews must be substantial, and in all likelihood dominant."

The website, *DNA Consultants*, which is a professional internet site for DNA science professionals and researchers, recently gave Koestler the ultimate, if belated, compliment in an article entitled, *"Khazarian Hypothesis or European Jewish Origins Vindicated."* The article says that the definitive DNA genetics research of Dr. Eran Elhaik of Johns Hopkins Medical University shows that Koestler's "Thirteenth Tribe" theory is correct. Then it goes on to say:

"A new study by Eran Elhaik (*Genome Biology and Evolution*, vol. 5.1, pp. 61-74) bears out our thinking with hard evidence that seems likely to settle that rancorously fought for question once and for all...

According to *Science News* (Jan 16, 2013), the new study sets to rest previous contradictory reports of Jewish ancestry. Elhaik's findings strongly support the Khazarian Hypothesis...

That's an entirely different version of history, one much closer to Arthur Koestler's account, a theory for which he was castigated by fellow

Jews and especially Zionists..."

According to both *DNA Consultants* and *Science News*, Elhaik's findings are scientifically valid and strongly convincing because of his superior methodology:

"The new study was not possible until recently, when many of the gaps in Caucasian and Jewish genetics were filled for the first time, using autosomal approaches rather than sex-linked haplotype surveys. Elhaik's masterwork examines a comprehensive dataset of 1,287 unrelated individuals in 8 Jewish and 74 non-Jewish populations genotyped over a range of half a million single nucleotide polymorphisms (SNPs) or markers. These data were adapted from a study by Doron Behar and colleagues from three years ago.

The central role of Khazaria was also not wanted or wished for among Eurocentric scholars, who tended to denigrate *Ostjuden* or Eastern Jews. Few historians conceded even the fact that Khazaria was a Jewish state that lasted nearly a millennium, where Hebrew was spoken, preferring to think of it as a sort of travelers tale or land of religious fiction.

"Elhaik used seven measures of ancestry, relatedness, admixture, allele sharing distances, geographical origins and migration patterns to identify the Caucasus-Near Eastern and European ancestral signatures in European Jews' genome along with a smaller, but substantial Middle Eastern genome. The results were consistent in depicting a Caucasus (Khazar) ancestry for all European Jews."

So Koestler and others were correct. The vast majority of "Jews" today come from the Khazaria emigration into Eastern Europe. They are not the descendants of Abraham. There was no mass migration (the "Wandering Jew" concept is a fraud) from Palestine at any time. The peoples of the Middle East that are now Palestinians, Shlomo Sand contends, were originally Judeans (or Jews). Over the years, these Judeans were assimilated into the local populations and became Moslems. This is why Dr. Ariella Oppenheim found in 2001 that so many of todays Palestinians have at least a small portion of Jewish DNA.

Newsflash! Palestinians have more ancient Israelite blood than do those today who say are Jews. And some have the "Cohen" chromosome Y to boot!

Amazingly, amazon.com shows there are at least six books on their list, all written by Jews, which use Oppenheim's research to claim that the Jews *are* "God's Chosen." Some of the authors reference Oppenheim's findings, focusing exclusively on the data indicating that some Jews have the "Cohen" DNA syndrome Y. This is their *proof.* The authors fail to mention that the Arabs and Palestinians have the same genetic markers in their blood. Moreover, they conveniently neglect Oppenheim's findings that the Jews are of Turkic/ Mongol stock.

DNA Science Is Indisputable

Science is not a light bulb. It does not change things instantly. But DNA science is indisputable, and over time—even as the

Christian Zionists and their friends, the Jewish rabbis, howl and vigorously protest—it becomes known and accepted.

Today, criminal juries find DNA reports convincing and powerful as evidence. The same measure of confidence is posited by the DNA research of Dr. Elhaik and his associates. We can expect much opposition to his scientific findings but in the end, truth will come out. Indeed, the truth is here now for anyone with eyes to read.

SEVEN

"All Hail the Jewish Master Race!"

"Pride goeth before destruction, and an haughty spirit before a fall."
— *Proverbs 16:18*

If I asked you what group of people embrace a set of doctrines declaring theirs the Master Race, what would your answer be? Most of you would probably answer, *"The Nazis."* Today, in fact, it is Jews who make poisonous claims to racial superiority. No, not *all* the Jews. But, as I will document, a huge number of leaders among the Jews ascribe to these wicked and dangerous theories of racial and blood superiority. Yet, in fact, DNA science proves conclusively that there is no Jewish race and that the Jews of today descended from Khazaria. The supposed Jews are not Jews at all, but are Khazars. They are *not* the seed of Abraham.

No Basis for Peace

In his memoirs of his years in the White House, former

79

President Jimmy Carter wrote that there could have been peace between the Arabs and the Israelis had it not been for the bigoted and mistaken racial views of Israeli's Prime Minister Menachem Begin. Begin, Carter recalled, believed the Jews were a Master Race, a holy people superior to Egyptians and Arabs. Begin also believed that God wanted the Jews to own the land, so there was absolutely no basis for peace. The Jews lusted after the land and intended to have it. Period.

Jews a Totally Different Species?

Rabbi Mendel Schneerson, the late Jewish Lubavitcher and friend of the senior George Bush, also believed the Jews are a superior Master Race. Many Jews today agree with the late Rabbi. Some even believe that Schneerson will himself someday be resurrected and return as the Jewish World Messiah. Schneerson once explained his theory of Jewish racial superiority this way. He said,

> "We have a case of the Jew...a totally different species.
>
> The body of a Jewish person," Schneerson bragged, "is of a totally different quality from the body of members of all other nations of the world. Bodies of the Gentiles are in vain. An even greater difference is in regard to the soul...A non-Jewish soul comes from three satanic spheres, while the Jewish soul stems from holiness."

Holocaust activist Elie Wiesel, whose lies about his holocaust experiences seem to be legion, also claims that Jews are a superior race. *"Everything about us is different,"* Wiesel boasts. *"Jews are ontologically exceptional."*

Again, I point out that DNA science proves that this Jewish chest-beating and bragging of racial superiority is based on myths and fable, not on science and fact.

No Mixed Marriages for the Superior Race, and Other Discrimination

This poisonous theory of the Jews impacts their relations with all other nations and peoples. Because they are convinced they are the Master Race, superior, god souls living amongst inferior beasts, Israel does not sanction or allow mixed marriages (*The Jerusalem Report*, October 20, 1994, p.26). In the U.S.A., liberal Jews scream out for more mixed marriages, but only among Gentiles! Jewish leaders fund civil rights organizations and are in favor of increased immigration of foreign races. But back home in Israel, the Sharon government is now building a Berlin-style wall creating an apartheid nation, to keep "inferior" Gentiles in their segregated ghettos.

Ze'ev Chafeto, the courageous Jewish editor of *The Jerusalem Report* magazine, notes that Israeli laws harshly prohibit people of non-Jewish races from immigrating to Israel. The Jews are determined to keep their race "pure" and unblemished, just as the Nazis sought for the Aryans. Christians are especially not welcome, and Israelis frequently use words similar to the condescending slang word "nigger" to describe Christians and Gentiles—vulgar, Yiddish slur words like *"shiksa," "schwartze,"* and *"shegetsz."*

Since the Jews are claimed to be the Master Race, whose souls are said by the Talmud to be on a far higher plane than the animalistic, "satanic souls" of Gentiles, it is common for Jewish authorities to brand all Gentiles by the derogatory Yiddish term *"goy,"* a term akin to a curse word. Meanwhile, Arabs are deemed so inferior they are even lower than the goy.

Jewish Blood vs. Inferior Blood

When several of his students were accused of murdering a teenage Arab girl, Rabbi Yitzhak Ginsburg insisted: *"Jewish blood is not the same as the blood of a (Gentile) goy."* In other words, if a god-like Jew kills an inferior goy, how can that be murder?

Israeli Yeshiva (school) students often demonstrate and chant, *"Death to the Arabs."* Defending their extreme behavior, Rabbi Ido Elba explains, *"According to the Talmud, one may kill any Gentile."* Rabbi Schlomo Aviner adds that normal human codes and laws of justice and righteousness do not apply to the Jews.

The widely studied Gush Emunim holds that, *"Jews are not and cannot be a normal people...The Covenant made between God and the Jewish people effectively nullifies moral laws that bind normal nations."*

"Jesus a Bastard," says Jewish Talmud

Even the leaders of *Israel My Glory*, a fanatically pro-Zionist, supposedly Christian ministry, have made note of the bizarre views of the Jews as found in their own book of laws and traditions, the Jewish Talmud. The organization's magazine (Dec./Jan. 1995/1996) published a revealing article detailing many of the hate-filled Talmudic beliefs of the Rabbis and their Zionist followers.

These beliefs include the teaching that Jesus was born a bastard and his mother, Mary, was a harlot *(Mishna Yebamoth 4,13)*; that Jesus practiced black arts of magic *(Sanhedrin 1076)*, and that Jesus is now suffering eternal punishment in a boiling vat of filthy excrement *(Mishna Sanhedrin X, 2)*. These references come from the English translation of the Talmud known as *The Soncino Talmud*.

Indeed, the anti-Christian movie, *The Last Temptation of Christ*, produced by Universal Studios and its Chairman, the Jew, Lewis Wasserman, was an accurate, if disgusting, reflection of what the Jews' most holy book, the *Talmud*, teaches. And yet the Rabbis and leaders of the Jewish-led Simon Wiesenthal Center, the ADL, and the Southern Poverty Law Center had the audacity to blast and criticize Mel Gibson's movie, *The Passion*, merely because it recounts the gospel truth about the trial and death of Jesus. What hypocrites!

Memory of Jesus to be Blotted Out

The Talmud is full of language that portrays the Jews as God's Master Race and depicts all other races as trash and garbage. It warns Jews to stay away from Christians because Christians are said to be *"unclean"* and *"murderers."*

On the other hand, a Jew is pictured as one of God's Chosen People. The Jew is said to possess so great a dignity that no one, not even an angel, can share equality with him. In fact, the Jew is said to be the equal of God. Rabbi Chanina says that, *"He who strikes an Israelite acts as if he slaps the face of God's Divine Majesty."* Because the Christian is considered unclean, a murderer, and an idolater, he must be exterminated, slaughtered without pity, squashed like a bug. *"The memory of that man (Jesus) should be forever blotted out."*

But Jesus is only the first of many Christians that are to be killed, says the Talmud. The famous Jewish rabbi, Maimonides, acclaimed by Christian apologists and defenders of Zionism as "a great man of God," encouraged Jews to kill all Christians. In the Talmud *(Hilkoth Akrum, X, 1)*, Maimonides says, *"Do not have pity for them. Show no mercy unto them. Therefore, if you see one in difficulty of drowning, do not go to his help... it is right to kill him by your own hand by shoving him into a well or in some other way."*

The monstrous and barbaric treatment Israel gives to Palestinians and other Arabs taken prisoner is easily understood when we realize that the Jews' own holy book, the Talmud, commands that heretics and traitors be killed without delay *(Abhodah Zarah, 266)* and that a Gentile taken prisoner may be killed, *"even before he confesses...the sooner the better"* *(Choschen Hammischpat, 388, 10).*

Murder of Gentiles Praised as a "Holy Sacrifice"

Moreover, the murder of Gentiles by Jews is said by the Talmud to be a *"holy sacrifice"* to God *(Zohar, III, 2276 and I, 38b and 39a).* Death of Gentiles by beheading is especially recommended *(Pesachim, 49b).*

The award-winning Jewish propaganda movie, *Schindler's List*, depicts Schindler lamenting how few Jews he has been able to save from a Nazi labor camp. But a little, old Jewish man says to him, "In our holy book, the Talmud, it says that if you save just one life, it is as if you have saved the entire world." Actually, the exact wording in the Talmud says that if you save just one *Jewish* life, it is as if you have saved the entire world. According to the Talmud, Gentile lives, of course, have little value.

It is important to remember that, to the Jews, the Talmud is not an obsolete and crusty document. The rabbis teach that it is a living and breathing instructional document, a modern-day, indispensable holy book. U.S. Supreme Court Justice Ruth Bader Ginsburg, an ardent Jewish believer, was quoted in *The New York Times* as giving credit to the Talmud for her success on the bench. *"The Talmud,"* said Ginsburg, *"is my sacred guide for daily living."*

Children Raped and Murdered

In Rome, Italy, in 2000, Italian police broke up a ring of eleven top Jewish gangsters. It was discovered that they had been kidnapping Gentile (non-Jewish) children between the ages of two and five from orphanages, raping them, and then murdering the children. These despicable crimes were recorded live on film and sold throughout the infamous global "snuff film" industry. Over 1,700 customers had paid as much as $20,000 per film to view little children being raped and murdered.

Both the *Associated Press* and *Reuters* agencies reported this heinous crime on September 27, 2000 (Also see *The Rome Observer*, October 1, 2000). But *few* U.S. newspapers and *none* of America's TV news networks carried this shocking news story. Why?

When Italian TV broadcast scenes of the arrests of the snuff film perverts at prime time to more than eleven million viewers, Jewish officials went berserk. Claiming "blood libel," they demanded that the Jewish elite who sat on the board of directors of the Italian TV network punish those responsible for allowing this news to surface. It was done. The TV executives were fired.

One cannot help but wonder: Was it Judaism's most holy book, the Talmud, that put it in the hearts of those monsters to commit such brutish and evil crimes against children? After all, their Talmud says that if a grown man rapes a young girl under three years of age, *"it is nothing."* And Gentiles, according to the Talmud, may be killed practically without restriction.

The Master Race—Beyond Good and Evil

In any event, the supposed Jewish Master Race cannot be held to normal standards of righteousness and morality. They are said to be *"beyond good and evil."* That is what thousands of Jewish rabbis and Illuminists believe about the Jews.

When questioned about his earlier role in the genocidal

massacre by Israeli defense forces of thousands of unarmed Egyptian POWs during the 1973 Arab-Israeli war, Prime Minister Yitzak Rabin snapped, *"I'm not going to discuss that. That's ancient history."* An odd and telling comment, indeed, since the Jews insist there is no statute of limitations that prevents the capture, trial, and execution of Germans accused of war crimes that occurred in the 1930s and 1940s, over six decades ago.

"Ye Shall Die Like Men"

God is not a racist. He has no use for haters. In the Holy Bible, our Saviour totally refutes and condemns the heinous and unconscionable Master Race theory, confirming to us that there is nothing holy in men's flesh and blood: *"Now this I say, brethren, that flesh and blood cannot inherit the kingdom of God"* (1 Corinthians 15:50).

In the Bible, King David flatly told the unrighteous Jews that even though by tradition they claimed they were gods, *"ye shall die like men"* (Psalm 82:1-8).

Gilad Atzmon, the famous Jazz musician, himself a Jew, has written a book discussing the illegitimate racial claims of the Jews. It's title: *The Wandering Who.*

Further amplifying this point, Martin Vellum, noted Estonian archaeologist and genetics researcher states: "No court would rule that a person is a Jew."

Divine Blood of the Master Race

The Jews fervently believe their blood is divine, and that only the Jews comprise a Holy Nation. They view themselves as "God's Chosen," a special Master Race. Their Zionist leaders smugly view other peoples as vermin, as inferior and of little value. The Jews and their leaders are sadly mistaken. They are in dire need of instruction and repentance.

EIGHT

The Children of Pride Belong to the Synagogue of Satan

Who Are the Jews?...Who are the Imposters?

"In those days came John the Baptist, preaching in the wilderness of Judaea...But when he saw many of the Pharisees and Sadducees come to his baptism, he said unto them, O generation of vipers, who hath warned you to flee from the wrath to come?"
—Matthew 3:1,7

"But avoid foolish questions, and genealogies, and contentions, and strivings about the law; for they are unprofitable and vain."
—Titus 3:9

W*ho are the Jews?* What a simple question. It also has a simple answer. Tragically, however, few people have discovered this

87

simple answer, and the consequences have been that over the decades and millennia, hundreds of millions of innocent men, women, and children have been tortured, beaten, raped, and murdered. Their homes and property have been stolen and the entire world has been filled with pain, tears, and bloodshed.

These crimes have been perpetrated by evil men and women who say they are Jews and who believe that their God sanctions their criminality because they are His Chosen People. To these Jews, their genealogy is of utmost importance. But the Bible points out that to emphasize genealogies is foolish, unprofitable, and in vain! *(Titus 3:9)*

In fact, now that it is demonstrated by conclusive DNA evidence that the current-day Jews are *not* the seed of Abraham, the contention that their genealogy is vitally important is dissolved. The Jews are Khazars; they have *no* Israelite heritage whatsoever.

Is it any wonder, therefore, that the Apostle Paul so wisely advised: "But avoid foolish genealogies, and contentions, and strivings about the law; for they are unprofitable and vain."

This advice, mind you, came from a *real Jew*, a born again Apostle of Jesus Christ, who physically was an Israelite of the Tribe of Benjamin. His advice, once again, is to *"avoid foolish genealogies..."* He well knew that God searched the reins of every man's heart regardless of their race or national origin.

We find, then, that God abhors those who exalt the flesh and that Paul advises us not to waste time on "foolish genealogies." The DNA science of scholars like Dr. Eran Elhaik should put an end to such contentions. Interestingly, most Christians today are *not* Zionists and some have long held the view that the Jews are not God's Chosen People.

Take Evangelist John Bray, a strong Baptist, whose book, *Israel in Bible Prophecy* (now published by American Vision, P.O. Box 220, Powder Springs, GA, 30127), sited the

Khazarian-Jewish link years before the definitive DNA research by Dr. Elhaik. Bray states:

"The majority of these so-called Jews in the world today are not blood-Jews, but in the majority are the descendants of the Khazars. Khazaria, home of the Khazars, was once the largest country in that whole area (the southern part of the old U.S.S.R. empire), and their people converted to Judaism; and as time went on these so-called Jews immigrated to Poland and Lithuania where the majority of Jews were at that time..."

Satan and his human cohorts do not want you, me, and the rest of humanity to know the simple and honest answer to this simple question, *"Who are the Jews?,"* and so they have come up with fabrications, deceit, and lies as the answer. These lies have been the fuel used by Communists and Zionists to empower evil and stage the most barbaric, unspeakable, fiendish of crimes which they justify by even more lies.

The Synagogue of Satan is Responsible For Mass Deaths and Misery

The Bible's book of *Revelation* warns that many more deaths and horrible crimes of barbarism are to occur. The prophecies even finger and identify the ones who will be guilty of this grim carnage of death and misery. In *Revelation 2* and *3*, God clearly and forthrightly reveals who these genocidal mass killers are—He calls them the *"Synagogue of Satan."*

I repeat: It is the *Synagogue of Satan* that shall throw innocents in prison and bring such horror and tribulation upon the world. What's more, God even goes so far as to define who it is that comprises this monstrous religious sect, He states: *"I know the blasphemy of them which say they are Jews and are not, but are the synagogue of Satan" (Revelation 2:9).*

In *Revelation 3:8-9,* God again speaks of these evildoers, whom he says are *"them of the synagogue of Satan, which say they are Jews, and are not, but do lie."*

They Say They Are Jews, But They Lie

The Synagogue of Satan is made up of Satan-possessed wicked people who say they are *Jews.* By this, by saying they are Jews, these people are claiming special rights as the spiritual descendants of Abraham. These "Jews" boast they are God's Chosen, and claim they are heirs to the promises given Abraham. Many believe it is their spiritual destiny to reign and rule over the Gentiles in a Jewish Kingdom yet to come. *They are horribly mistaken.*

In fact, being *spiritual* imposters, they are *not* God's Chosen. They are either mistaken or they are *lying!*

Oh the wonders of our God! How I do love the fact that He confuses the wicked who are proud in their own minds. And at the same time, our marvelous God reveals the truth to His saints. The people of the Evil One are unable to unravel the profound *mysteries of God,* because these mysteries are *spiritually discerned.* As Paul explains in the New Testament, the unsaved person is carnal—of the flesh—he or she is a natural-born person but has not been *spiritually* born again. But the "natural man," says the Apostle, cannot discern the things of God:

> *"For to be carnally minded is death; but to be spiritually minded is life and peace. Because the carnal mind is enmity against God: for it is not subject to the law of God, neither indeed can be. So*

then they that are in the flesh cannot please God."
(Romans 8:6-9)

I am sorry, dear unsaved Ph.D. holder, your credentials and your highly esteemed (by the world) diplomas will be of no use to you in deciphering the mysteries of God. You shall languish in ignorance, no matter if your degree certificate comes from even the most prestigious of institutions—Yale, Harvard, Princeton, MIT, or Rice. Unless you are changed into a *new person* by the power of God through faith in Jesus Christ, you are consigned to permanent residence at Satan's University of Confusion.

Who, Then, is a Spiritual "Jew?"

Now, for those who have ears to hear and eyes to see, let us answer that probing question, *"Who are the Jews?"* We go direct to the scriptures to do so. First, to *Romans 2:28-29*:

"For he is not a Jew, which is one outwardly; neither is that circumcision, which is outward in the flesh:

But he is a Jew, which is one inwardly; and circumcision is that of the heart, in the spirit, and not in the letter; whose praise is not of men, but of God."

The Apostle Paul wanted us to clearly understand this key principle—that being a "Jew" and being of the *Promise* has nothing to do with the flesh or with outward appearance. Being physically born as a "Jew" is totally irrelevant for there are *two* Israels—the Israel of the flesh, which is in bondage to Satan, and the Israel of God, which is free and is of Jesus

Christ. Here is what Paul had to say in *Romans 9:6-8* and *24*:

> *"For they are not all Israel, which are of Israel:*
> *Neither, because they are the seed of Abraham, are*
> *they all children (of God)...*
>
> *That is, they which are the children of the flesh,*
> *these are not the children of God: but the children of*
> *the promise are counted for the seed...*
>
> *Even us, whom he hath called, not of the Jews only,*
> *but also of the Gentiles?"*

Being a "Jew," then, according to God, has nothing to do with being a Jew in the flesh. Instead, a true Jew is a person who has faith in Christ Jesus. He is thus born again and is spiritually a new person.

> *"Therefore it is of faith, that it might be by grace; to*
> *the end the promise might be sure to all the seed;...*
> *which is of the faith of Abraham; who is the father*
> *of us all,*
>
> *As it is written, I have made thee a father of many*
> *nations... Now it was not written for his sake*
> *alone,... But for us also... if we believe on him that*
> *raised up Jesus our Lord from the dead;*
>
> *Therefore being justified by faith, we have peace*
> *with God through our Lord Jesus Christ." (Romans*
> *4 and 5)*

How splendid is that! A true Jew is that spiritually reborn person who has faith in Jesus. In fact, the true Jew is a citizen of heavenly Jerusalem, also known as Zion, the heavenly City of God. He is a child of God and the children of God may come from any race or nation, because Abraham was made *"father of many nations."* That promise was also given (see *Genesis 12*) to Abraham's "seed." And who might that be? Well Abraham's seed are all those men and women—of Jewish or Gentile DNA—who believe in God and that He raised up Jesus from the dead.

A person who is a Jew by flesh does not possess the promise given to Abraham unless he has faith in Jesus. He is not the heir. He is not one of God's Chosen. And if he says he is, he is an imposter and a liar.

Christians, not Physical Jews, Are God's Chosen

Thus—listen closely, please—if you have faith in Jesus Christ, if you are His, then you are a child of God. Your physical race or bloodline is of absolutely no significance because, as the Apostle Peter states, it is Christians who come *out* of many nations who are now One Holy Nation. They are the Chosen of God and are the children of God:

> *"But ye are a chosen generation, a royal priesthood, an holy nation, a peculiar people; that ye should shew forth the praises of him who hath called you out of darkness into his marvellous light." (1 Peter 2:9)*

Now that really puts an end to any kind of racism, doesn't it, including the toxin-producing Jewish Supremacism of today's physical Jews. Physical Jews today, whether they reside in Israel, the U.S.A., or elsewhere, say they are of their father Abraham. They use this claim to commit all manner of crimes, including the ethnic cleansing of Palestine. Many evangelical Christians agree with them.

But, hold on. God does not honor their bogus claim because he does not honor or esteem a person's fleshly origins. The "Jews" of today say they are the seed, but what the scriptures affirm is that only Christians (Jew or Gentile bloodline) are the seed of Abraham. Want proof? Ok, read these lovely verses in *Galatians 3:7-29*:

> *"Know ye therefore that they which are of faith, the same are the children of Abraham...*
>
> *That the blessing of Abraham might come on the Gentiles through Jesus Christ; that we might receive the promise of the Spirit through faith...*
>
> *Now to Abraham and his seed were the promises made...*
>
> *There is neither Jew nor Greek, there is neither bond nor free, there is neither male nor female: for ye are all one in Christ Jesus.*
>
> *And if ye be Christ's, then are ye Abraham's seed, and heirs according to the promise."*

Throw Out the Flesh!

Throw out the flesh! Flesh cannot inherit the kingdom of God. Flesh shall grow corrupt and return to dust. God doesn't give any preference to a person based on the circumstances of his physical birth. Only what is *spirit* will survive and go on into destiny. As Christ told Nicodemus, "A man must be *born again* in spirit and in truth" *(John 3:3)*.

Those who, filled with human pride, say they are "Jews"

and claim in their Talmud that they are superior to the *goyim* (cattle; i.e.—Gentiles) are ignorant of the fact that even if they are of the Jewish race—and DNA science proves conclusively that the vast majority of so called "Jews" even lie about that, their flesh will do them no good: The scriptures wisely warn: "For if ye live after the flesh, ye shall die..." *(Romans 8:13)*.

The Talmud, the most holy book of the physical Jews, is satanic to the core. It is a set of hateful and ridiculous volumes invented by demonic rabbis. The true scriptures—the Holy Bible—testify that if a person has not the Spirit of God, he is not *of* God, but instead belongs to his father, Satan *(Romans 8)*. The Devil is chief of all the "children of pride" *(Job 41)*.

The Natural Born Jew is Just A Human Being—Nothing More!

The natural man cannot discern the things of God. This scriptural doctrine is true. Only the spiritual man redeemed by Christ Jesus has the God-given wisdom to discern the things

The Jewish Talmud's many volumes.

of God. The natural-born Jew is, simply put, just another human being in need of redemption through Jesus Christ. Nothing more.

The prideful Jews bragged to Jesus that Abraham was their father, that they were his seed. But Jesus came right back at them and told the physical Jews that Satan, not Abraham, was their father. Likewise, today's Jews and their Judaizer/Zionist accomplices make the same false claim.

Spiritual Jews Believe in Jesus

These are physical "Jews" and are not *spiritual Jews (Revelation 3:8-9)*. If they were Abraham's children, they would believe in Jesus! Jesus said so. Christ admitted they were the *physical* seed of Abraham, but explained that this means absolutely nothing to God.

That is why Jesus, hearing their prideful boast of having Abraham as their father, told those who said they were Jews that even though they were the physical seed of Abraham, they were not truly heirs and were not blessed with Abraham as their father. The blessing is *spiritual* in nature, not carnal.

Hey Judaizer...and you, Zionist!—Did you read that? Jesus said that men and women who say they are Jews due only to their flesh's heritage are wrong. They are *not* true Jews, and Abraham is not their spiritual father. Jesus flatly told them, "ye are of your father the devil." So if you are helping these imposters to build up a Kingdom of God on earth (physical Israel), you are helping the Devil. How's that working out?

And so today, when a Goldstein, a Silverton, a Rothschild, a Streisand, a Soros, or a Netanyahu boast, "I am a Jew. I am the seed of my father, Abraham," well, Jesus has a piercingly sharp message for you, *"No you are not! You are of your Father the devil, and his works you will do. He was a liar and a murderer and so are you."*

A Generation of Vipers

No wonder Jesus' forerunner, John the Baptist, scoffed at the Pharisees and Sadducees who came to him saying they wanted to be baptized.

"Ye generation of vipers, who hath warned you to flee from the wrath to come?

Bring forth therefore fruits meet for repentance.

And think not to say within yourselves, we have Abraham as our Father, for I say unto you, that God is able of these stones to raise up children unto Abraham.

And now the ax is laid unto the foot of the trees: therefore every tree which bringeth not forth good fruit is hewn down and cast into the fire." (Matthew 3:7-10)

Have the Judaizers and Zionists not read these verses? Do they not see nor understand that the people—and race—which boasts they are "Jews" and are "Abraham's seed"—and are implying this automatically gives them spiritual superiority and standing with God—are *imposters*. They spiritually are liars and vipers. God did not and does not care one whit what your bloodline is, or your flesh type, or your genotype, or your DNA.

Give no regard also to any notion of genealogical superiority. God scorns this as foolishness. He doesn't give a fig if you are Celtic, Israeli, Arab, Mexican, or a Heinz 57 mixture!

Every man, every woman who has Jesus as Lord is

Abraham's seed and is heir to the promise given Abraham. And not because of race, heritage, or outward appearance. But because, as John the Baptist so sagely stated: *"God is able of these stones to raise up children unto Abraham."*

Paul says that God broke down the wall, or partition, between Jews and Gentiles. From the moment Jesus died on the cross for all our sins—and rose in triumph—the true Jew has been he who is blessed with eternal life because of his faith in the Saviour, Jesus Christ.

Jews and Gentiles Need Jesus

Know this: That the person who says he is a Jew *solely* due to birth and race (i.e. *flesh*) but rejects Jesus is *not* a citizen of the Israel of God, but is an *imposter*. Neither does such a person know God or belong to Him. He or she may be of the physical bloodline of Abraham or he may be a Khazar. But, if so, who cares? God certainly does not.

The physical Jew, like natural men and women of *all* nations, is separated from God by his sin and needs the redeemer, Jesus Christ. Unless Jesus is their Lord and Saviour, physical Jews and Gentiles alike are the property of Satan, their father.

The true seed of Abraham, then, is the Christian, for the promise of salvation and glory is not of race, but of faith and grace. God's children have been raised up out of all nations and pressed into the Kingdom of God. They are indeed the "Israel of God" *(Galatians 6)*, not the Israel of planet earth whose citizens belong to their father, Satan.

Exalt Not the Natural Man

My counsel is that you and I exalt not the natural man, but praise God for the spiritual man who has Christ within. If any man does not understand this truth, he is not of God.

NINE

He Came Out of Babylon...

Was Abraham a Jew?

"Now to Abraham and his seed were the promises made. He (God) saith not, And to seeds, as of many; but as of one, And to thy seed, which is Christ."
—Galatians 3:16

"They which are the children of the flesh, these are not the children of God: But the children of the promise are counted as the seed."
—Romans 9:8

Was Abraham, the biblical patriarch, a Jew? Many Christians believe that Abraham was, indeed, of Jewish blood. Christians who believe this also say that if Abraham can be proven to be a Jew, then the Jews living today are his "seed," his racial

99

descendants. As such, it is claimed that, as Abraham's seed and heirs, Jews today are entitled to the promises made to Abraham long ago by God.

However, if it turns out that Abraham was *not* born a Jew, then big, big troubles emerge. Does that mean that his "seed" today are not the Jews, but some other tribe, race, or people? And if Abraham wasn't born a Jew, who then has the divine right to possess the land of Palestine? Today's Jews fanatically claim this territory theirs by heirdom and divine birthright. But, are modern-day Jews interlopers on the land? Are they nothing more than illegitimate squatters, or worse? Are they robbers and thieves who unlawfully have taken someone else's property?

Shocker!—Abraham a Babylonian

It often comes as a shock to unaware Christians to discover that Abraham did not come from some Jewish family that practiced a religion called "Judaism." He was not born in some kind of Jewish ghetto town, village, province or nation. Abraham, in fact, was a native-born *Babylonian!*

Yes, that's right. Abraham came originally from the same nation where, previously, Nimrod and Semiramis and their builders had attempted to build the failed Tower of Babel. Babylon...wicked, wicked Babylon.

Genesis 11:31 says that Abraham (then named Abram) and his father, Terah, left their home in Ur of the Chaldees to go into the land of Canaan, where they took up residence in the city of Háran. Ur of the Chaldees is a city in what was then called Babylon. Today, Ur is in Iraq.

Why did Abraham leave Ur, this city in ancient Babylon? The Lord had said unto Abraham, "Get thee out of thy country and from thy kindred unto a land that I will shew thee..." *(Genesis 12:1).*

Notice here that the *"kindred"* of Abraham were the people who lived in Ur, that is, in Babylon, also known as Mesopotamia (see *Acts 7:1-4*).

So the scriptures tell us that Abraham came from Mesopotamia, e.g. Babylon. Nothing in the scriptures says he was a "Hebrew" or a "Jew."

Abraham Father of *"Many Nations"*

Now, while Abraham did come out of Babylon, where his kindred resided, it is interesting that God told Abraham:

> *"...in thee shall all families of the earth be blessed."*
> *(Genesis 12:3)*

> *"...thou shalt be a father of many nations"* *(Genesis 17:2-9)*

Here we find an amazing prophetic fact. Abraham was chosen by God to be much more than merely the father of a geographically limited nation-state in the Middle East area. Abraham's destiny is far greater than that. God promised Abraham he would be father of *many* nations and that *all the families of the earth* would be blessed by his "seed."

In fact, it is the seed of Abraham who are heirs of the promises of God. The key to understanding the entire Word of God is wrapped up in understanding *who* is the seed of Abraham. Jesus once declared that if a man were to understand the mystery of the seed, his sins would be forgiven him and he would be saved! *(Mark 4:11-13)*

The Seed of Abraham Discovered

So, *who is the seed of Abraham?* Don't ask most pastors and preachers this question, because they *don't* know! And they *don't want* to know! However, Paul provided us the answer in *Galatians:*

> *"Now to Abraham and his seed were the promises made. He saith not, And to seeds, as of many; but as of one, And to thy seed, which is Christ."*

> *"For ye are all the children of God by faith in Christ Jesus. For as many of you as have been baptized into Christ have put on Christ. There is neither Jew nor Greek, there is neither bond nor free, there is neither male nor female: for ye are all one in Christ Jesus."*

What a revelation! Note that, according to Paul, the seed is *not* a physical race of people because flesh cannot inherit the kingdom of heaven. It matters not whether a person is Jew or Gentile—God gives no preference. *John 3:3* says that the seed, that is, the chosen of God, must be born again in spirit and in truth, not in the flesh.

Finally, Jesus Himself identified this seed when he stated, "Now the parable is this: The seed is the Word of God" *(Luke 8:11).* And who is the Word of God? *John 1* reveals that the Word of God is Jesus Christ, the eternal Word of God.

In sum, the seed is the Word of God, and the Word of God is Christ Jesus. So, if you belong to Christ, *you* are the seed of Abraham. That's why the Apostle Paul wrote, "And if ye be Christ's, then are ye Abraham's seed and heirs according to the promise" *(Galatians 3:29).* Thus, do not burden yourself with the foolishness of genealogies. It matters not of what race Abraham was or what race *you* and I are today. Citizenship in God's Kingdom through faith in Jesus is all that matters. All praises to the Kingdom of God and to Jesus, the eternal King who sits on the throne!

We discover from the scriptures, then, that those who are Christ's are Abraham's seed and as such, they are heirs to the promise, which is the promise of eternal life through Jesus Christ our Lord.

The Israel of God—God Chooses A People Out of Many Nations

Back to Abraham: For those who unscripturally continue to parrot the Judaizer teaching that he was either a Jew or a Hebrew, I ask, should we even care about his physical genealogy or race? Consider...

- Paul wrote: *"Neither give heed to fables and endless genealogies, which minister questions, rather than Godly edifying which is in faith: so do." (1 Timothy 1:4)*

- Paul, referring to whether God favors Jews or Gentiles, also wrote: *"For there is no respect of persons with God." (Romans 2:11 and Romans 3: 9-10)*

- Paul further explained that being a *"Jew"* is not a matter of flesh, or race, but *"of the heart"* and of whether a person is *"in the spirit."*

- The promise given Abraham is given to the seed; that is to all the saved who are chosen out of *"many nations." (Romans 4:16-18)*

Paul, in *Galatians 6:16*, speaks of the "Israel of God." He is referring to the spiritual nation of Israel, made up of *all* (Jews or Gentile) who are saved through faith in Jesus.

God's Israel, therefore, is composed of Christians chosen

out of all the nations on earth. God's Israel is not solely a nation of physical Jews. Race or flesh has nothing to do with the "Israel of God." It is instead a spiritual nation of saved people who belong to Jesus, people white, black, red, yellow, brown. Listen to how the Apostle Peter describes this marvelous, God-created nation of Israel and its people:

"But ye are a chosen generation, a royal priesthood, an holy nation, a peculiar people...which in time past were not a people, but are now the people of God." (1 Peter 2:9-10)

"And So, All Israel Shall Be Saved."

There we have it. God's People are the spiritual seed of Abraham who are Christ's own. They are a "holy nation." In other words, they are Christ's Chosen People. He chooses them because of their faith in Him, and that alone! They comprise the spiritual nation of "Israel," no matter what their ethnic race, no matter what their geographic origin or nationality.

Greek Christians, American Christians, Jewish Christians, Mexican Christians—all are heavenly citizens of "Israel." All true believers are chosen to inherit the New Jerusalem, the heavenly City of God. In the New Jerusalem, there is no concept of "race," for all citizens of heavenly Zion are born again in spirit and in truth *(John 3:3)* through faith in Jesus, our Savior.

Now we understand why Paul wrote: *"And so, all Israel shall be saved (Romans 11:26)."* In other words, all who are in Christ Jesus, the Word of God, shall be saved, for they are Abraham's seed and heirs to the promise of eternal life. Believers in Christ comprise the holy nation of "Israel" and all are saved through faith in Christ Jesus. Again, the Word emphasizes: They are the seed by *faith*, not by race.

Abraham and the Prophets Look to "Heavenly Jerusalem"

Finally, we have the testimony of Abraham who considered his earthly inheritance (the land and territory given him by God) as nothing more than a temporary way-station, even "a strange country" *(Hebrews 10:11-16)*.

Are you an earthly citizen of the United States of America? Maybe you are an Israeli, a Palestinian, a German, a Lithuanian, or a Chinese? Maybe, like Abraham, you are an Iraqi, a "Babylonian."

The wonderful news is that our physical blood race or DNA has no significance at all as far as God is concerned. He is no respecter of persons. Whosoever will, may come. All who have faith in Jesus Christ are wayfarers and pilgrims in this world, and as such, we look up to heaven and to our eternal kingdom.

TEN

The Kingdom of God Given to Another Nation

Jesus Took the Kingdom From the Jews

"Therefore say I unto you, The kingdom of
God shall be taken from you, and given to a
nation bringing forth the fruits thereof."
                              —*Matthew 21:43*

Today, millions of Christian evangelicals, led by
their Zionist prophet, John Hagee, are dead-set
on helping the Jews conquer the Middle East.
They view it as their Christian duty to assist the Israelis to kill
and subjugate the Arab and Palestinian peoples.

But, are these evangelical Christians actually being conned
into helping build Satan's end-times global empire? As we
shall see, a terrible deception is at work here. This great
deception centers on a bizarre racial theory put forth by

evangelical teachers. These teachers—some of the biggest names in Christendom—are convinced that the Jewish nation, fleshly Israel, is destined to inherit the Kingdom of God based on their race alone.

Of course, this bizarre notion is wildly unscriptural, but where are the preachers today who pay any attention to what the scriptures really say? Where are the preachers who have the courage to tell the Jews the truth: *"Jesus has taken the Kingdom of God from you and given it to another nation bringing forth fruits?"*

This is exactly what Jesus said *(Matthew 21:43);* yet, few Pastors or other Christian teachers dare mention it, for fear of the Jews. They are fearful of being called "anti-Semitic" and are paralyzed by the likelihood of their being considered "politically incorrect."

Instead of preaching the truth, today's predominantly Judaizer, fanatically pro-Israel, Jewish supremacist evangelical ministers actually are teaching *exactly the opposite* of what Jesus and His apostles taught.

God's Majesty Too Awesome For Earth Alone

The fanatical goal today of both Zionist Jews and Judaizer Christian evangelicals is to build up a Jewish Kingdom here on earth, with Jerusalem, the Great City, as its capital. This carnal, worldly objective drives the Zionists and Judaizers ever onward.

Their aim of course, is to physically establish the throne of God in earthly Jerusalem and watch as a Jewish Messiah appears to reign over what they expect will be a 1000 year-long Jewish empire and dominion. Many are funding efforts to rebuild the Jewish temple in Jerusalem, which they expect will be a house and a place of rest for the Lord.

Apparently though, God has other plans. God, you see, is

Lord of the entire universe. His Glorious Kingdom is not limited to this puny planet. Why should he degrade His utter majesty and accept a mere earthly throne?

Yes, indeed, the earth is His, but so are trillions and trillions of other planets, stars, and other heavenly bodies, seen and unseen by human eyes. His Kingdom, His glory, are never ending. Amen.

"Wait just a minute," say the Zionist Jews and their Judaizer helpers-in-crime. "God is just lusting to sit on a dusty old throne in a temple built by human hands right here on earth. He even has a people—the Jews—who will rule and reign with Him. His throne is earthly, not infinite."

"God *needs* an earthly temple in Jerusalem," say Jewish Zionist and Gentile Judaizers; he requires a "house" and a throne here on this planet. The Zionists and Judaizers claim that Christians also need a rebuilt temple in Jerusalem, a holy place where Christians can celebrate Jewish feast days, sacrifice animals, and carry out Old Covenant Jewish rituals and ceremonies.

Just as the Zionist-inspired Scofield Bible teaches, the Jews and Christian evangelicals (Judaizers) are eager to establish their own worldly version of the *"Kingdom of God."* They are scheming and plotting to rebuild the ancient Jewish temple on the Temple Mount in Jerusalem. And anyone who dares suggest they are going in the wrong direction, they say, is just an anti-Semitic Jew-hater. So there!

"Heaven Is My Throne..."

Obviously, these fanatical Zionist advocates have failed to study the scriptures. Take *Acts 7:48-49*, for example, which instructs us:

> *"Howbeit the most High dwelleth not in temples*

made with hands; as saith the prophet,

*HEAVEN IS MY THRONE, AND EARTH IS MY
FOOTSTOOL: WHAT HOUSE WILL YE BUILD
ME? SAITH THE LORD: OR WHAT IS THE
PLACE OF MY REST?"*

Now that really should deflate the Jews, with all their excess human pride. They fancy themselves God's Chosen People and imagine that their earthly city, Jerusalem, and their earthly kingdom, Israel, is where God seeks to dwell forever. They really think that the Messiah will inhabit a Jewish flesh-and-blood body and sit on a throne built by human hands.

However, God's Word tells us clearly the opposite. This present day earth isn't a fit place for an omniscient all-powerful God to live and rest. No way. Heaven is His throne, say the scriptures, and earth is but his footstool.

I am so very thankful that Jesus our Lord and Saviour came as prophesied some 2,000 years ago as Emmanuel, God with us. How sweet and merciful of Him. Certainly, man is not worthy of His loving kindness.

I also appreciate the fact that He will someday return to rescue the saints and to destroy the Devil and his evil disciples. God has a *better place* than earth reserved for His saints. Mansions are waiting for us in Heaven. Praise God! Heaven is where His eternal throne is, and that's where I want to be. How about you, dear saints?

Regardless of the lies and confusion caused by the false teachings of the Judaizers, we know for sure that God's throne is in heaven. It will *not* be found in any earthly city, because God's Holy City is the *New Jerusalem*, a marvelously created metropolis that has no parallels at all with any filthy city made of dirt and brick here on earth. *The New Jerusalem, the heavenly City of God.* Oh what divine beauty is found in that magnificent abode.

This, then, is what the scriptures tell us, that Heaven is God's throne. Earth is but His footstool. Zionist Christians reject this and are working incessantly to set up His throne right here on earth, in earthly Jerusalem.

They seek, moreover, a Zionist Jewish Kingdom and are hotly demanding that the White House use American diplomacy and military firepower to assure these goals. Meanwhile, a militant and deadly Israel of the flesh, with U.S. taxpayer support, continues to oppress its enemies—Palestinians, Moslems, Arabs, Christians.

Opposing the Will of God

Sadly, Christian evangelicals are cheering them on, in eager anticipation of the soon coming of a mere man, an earthly Jewish King. They don't know it, but when such a man comes, his number will undoubtedly be 666, and he will go forth killing Christian believers and all who oppose his rule. But of this fact, the Zionists and Judaizers are totally, willfully ignorant. As Jesus prophesied, *"They will kill you and thinketh they do God service."*

Because of their hatred for Him and due to their rebellion, Jesus boldly announced to the Jews, *"Therefore I say unto you, The kingdom of God shall be taken from you and given to a nation bringing forth the fruits thereof" (Matthew 21:43).*

"No!" protest the Zionist and Christian Judaizers. "This cannot and will not stand. Christ made the wrong decision. He did a terrible thing in taking the kingdom from the Jews. We will undo what Christ has done. We will exalt the Jews. We will even praise them as God's eternal "Chosen People." They *will* possess the land. We will give the Jews the Kingdom. *Be gone Jesus. Our will be done!"*

Jews' House is Left Desolate

Significantly, today, Christian evangelicals and the neocons are working to build up the House of Israel, a House that Jesus tore down! Jesus prophesied that earthly Jerusalem would be destroyed and the temple thrown down stone by stone. And so it was, in 70 AD.

Jesus declared to the Jews, *"Behold, your house is left desolate. For I say unto you, Ye shall not see me henceforth, till ye shall say, Blessed is He that cometh in the name of the Lord" (Matthew 23:38-39).*

Yes, Jerusalem is *left desolate* until the moment that Jesus returns in glory. Has Jesus already returned? Did we miss His second coming? No, of course not. Yet, Christian Zionists apparently don't give one whit for what Jesus said. They seek to undo what Christ did. He threw down the Jews' temple. He made them outcasts from the land. He said that the House of Israel would be left desolate *until He returns.*

"No!" cry the arrogant and rebellious Zionists and Christian Judaizers (really Christian Zionists). "We will *not* listen to Christ. We *will* build up Jerusalem and Israel this very day and restore what Jesus tore down. We will make earthly Israel prosperous and strong, a great kingdom. We will not wait for Christ to return. We will *not* obey Him. There shall be *no more desolation.* Not His will, but our will be done."

A word of warning is surely in store for these rebellious, pro-Jewish zealots: *"Watch out! It's a dangerous thing to so callously oppose the will of Almighty God."*

"Sodom and Egypt" Praised and Helped by Christian Zionists

It gets worse. True it is that rebellious Christian Zionists are defying God's prophetic edict and are seeking to restore quickly the earthly House of Israel. But what is especially repulsive is that the Christian Zionists, in their willful disobedience, are actually laboring to recreate an unholy city that God describes in His Word as latter-day *"Sodom and Egypt."*

In fact, the scriptures clearly tell us that the last days, earthly city of Jerusalem, in Israel, will have become so wicked and vile that God Himself spiritually brands that city and its inhabitants as modern-day *"Sodom and Egypt."*

See for yourself: *Revelation 11:7-8* says that Jerusalem, the Great City, wherein our Lord was crucified, is spiritually *"Sodom and Egypt."* Think of it! Christian Zionists, disregarding everything that God said and did, are obsessed and consumed as they vainly pull out all stops to build here on earth a modern-day Jewish version of "Sodom and Egypt." How disgusted and sorrowful God must be at their stout effort to help the Devil and His disciples in Jerusalem build a 21st century "Sodom and Egypt." In reality, they are simply helping to create a cesspool fit only for final destruction. In fact, Christian Zionists are building up the new kingdom of Khazaria!

"Here We Have No Continuing City" (Hebrews 13:14)

While the Christian Zionists continually exalt Jerusalem as God's holy city—in defiance of the scriptures declaring this evil place "Sodom and Egypt," the fact is that the *real* holy city is *Heavenly Jerusalem*, the City of God, a fantastic citadel of glory built by the Lord as a habitat for his redeemed Christian saints.

The Christian evangelicals are joined by the Roman Catholic Church in their terrible error of confusing carnal and earthly things with spiritual treasures. The Pope, like the leaders of the evangelical churches (Southern Baptists,

Assembly of God, Pentecostals, *et al*) mistakenly believes the Old Covenant based on the Law is still in effect. But Paul explains that it has been replaced by the New Covenant of Jesus Christ, which he says is a *"new and better covenant" (Hebrews 8 and 9).*

The entire, flawed and rotten structure of pseudo-Christian Zionism thus comes crashing down. It is based on a covenant that, Paul wrote, *"decayeth and is vanishing."* The new and better covenant, however, is set firmly on the foundation of Jesus Christ, His resurrection, and His promises to His Chosen People, the redeemed Christians of all races and nations, who are collectively called God's nation, the "Israel of God" *(Galatians 4 and 6).*

In all this, as I demonstrate in my eye-opening video, *Illuminati Mystery Babylon*, the Jews and their evangelical adorers are unwittingly helping Satan set up a bloody empire. They are using their proxy, the United States, and its powerful military might to do so.

Zionists Strive to Nullify Jesus' Decision

It is tragic to discover so many people today claiming to be Christians who refuse to believe what the scriptures say about the Kingdom of God. Their failure to understand and follow the clear teachings of Jesus and the Apostles on spiritual Israel and the Kingdom makes me wonder if these deceived people are really even saved. Jesus taught his disciples that if a man were to understand, or know, the mystery of the Kingdom of God, he would be converted and his sins would be forgiven:

> *"And he said unto them, Unto you is given to know the mystery of the kingdom of God: but unto them that are without, all these things are done in parables:*

*That seeing they may see, and not perceive; and
hearing they may hear, and not understand; lest at
anytime they should be converted, and their sins
should be forgiven them." (Mark 4:11-12)*

What we have, then, is the United States being recruited by
Satan to build up his dark and wicked endtimes empire here on
earth. The *"Kingdom of God"* was taken away from the Jews
by Jesus. He declared their house would be left desolate. But
the last day's helpers of Satan, including the Christian Judaizer
evangelicals and the neocons, strive to nullify Jesus' decision.
The Jews *will* have their earthly kingdom, if the proud Zionists
and Judaizers have their way. Yes they shall. It will be a
kingdom all right—a kingdom for the Beast, the Son of
Perdition.

Christian Nation Given the Kingdom

If, as Jesus prophesied, the Kingdom has been taken from the
Jews, then to whom is it given? What of the Kingdom of God
that is promised? Jesus, in *Matthew 21:43*, declares that the
Kingdom of God will go not to the Jews of earthly Israel but
instead to *a nation* bringing forth fruits. What nation, then, is
given the kingdom? Which nation is bringing forth fruits?

Once again, the scriptures supply the answer. The Kingdom
of God was taken from the Jews and physical Israel and given
to Christians! *Christians are God's Chosen People*, and
Christians are His Holy Nation. The Apostle Peter wisely
addressed these matters. In *I Peter 2:4-6*, we read that
Christians—*not* Jews as a race—are *"chosen of God and
precious."* Peter instructed Christians:

*"...ye are a chosen generation, a royal priesthood,
an holy nation, a peculiar people... Which in time*

past were not a people, but are now the people of God." (1 Peter 2:9-10)

The above Bible verse, believe it or not, is hated and despised by many of today's evangelical leaders and church people. It totally destroys their man-made theories regarding Israeli superiority and Jewish racial supremacism. It elevates spiritual things over fleshly things. This they cannot accept.

These scriptures speak not of a physical race or of national origins, but of spiritual things. Christians are chosen out of *many* nations and spiritually are born again. In unity, all who are Christ's Chosen are the "people of God" and are "precious" in His sight, whether they be Jew or Gentile, German, African, Asian, Latino, Arab, English, or Italian. Only spirit matters.

Sad and tragic as it may be, the deceived Jews and their ungodly Judaizer evangelical associates will undoubtedly continue to build up Mystery Babylon. They will work and strive, heaping up treasure to insure its prosperity. In doing so, they simply assure their own destruction.

The scriptures reveal that their schemes, their plots, shall fail. One great day, the earth will be shaken, and all things that offend God will be removed *(Hebrews 12:25-27).*

Earthly Jerusalem, too, because it has become modern-day Sodom and Egypt, shall be removed and burned. But as for the Kingdom of God, it shall never fall. As the Apostle Paul so marvelously advised:

"Wherefore we receiving a kingdom which cannot be moved, let us have grace, whereby we may serve God acceptably with reverence and godly fear: for our God is a consuming fire." (Hebrews 12:28-29)

ELEVEN

Dispelling Centuries of Hate and Prejudice

Jesus and His Seed Revealed

"The seed of a Gentile is worth the same as that of a beast."
> —*Jewish Talmud (Kethobeth 36)*

It is ironic that the people of Israel and of World Jewry have been discovered by DNA science to be Khazars and not the seed of Abraham. It is befitting because, in their own holy book, the Talmud (the official name is the *Babylonian Talmud!*), we discover supreme hatred and prejudice against Gentiles. Of course, when the Talmud was written, the Khazars were heathen pagans who worshipped the phallus, the generative sex act, and nature spirits. But when the Khazars converted to Judaism in the 8th century, the Talmud became their guide to the new religion.

In fact, most rabbis spend not one minute in their yeshivas (religious schools) studying the Old Testament. Only the Talmud is studied, and it is often quoted by rabbis in their sermons and counseling.

The Khazar Jew—virtually all are now proven by DNA to be Khazars—is a Gentile, and yet he believes in the Talmud, which preaches that the Gentile has no soul, is a beast, and when the Jews receive the Kingdom will be killed if he refuses to be a slave and serve the Jew.

There is no dispute about how much the Jews venerate and respect their holy book, the Babylonian Talmud. First printed about 550 AD, today the Talmud is considered the ultimate source of Judaic doctrine and practice. U.S. Supreme Court Justice Ruth Bader Ginsburg told *The New York Times* the Talmud was her "guide for daily living."

Greater Than the Old Testament?

Most Christians assume that Judaism is based solely on the books of the Old Testament. Not so. The rabbis contend that the Talmud, a collection of commentaries and advisories about their 613 laws, actually is a greater authority than the Old Testament. In fact, inside the pages of the Talmud we discover that God actually consults the Talmud and the rabbi sages when *He* has a question or query about the law!

It is against the laws of Judaism, as expressed in the Talmud, for a Jew to teach a Gentile about the Talmud. Indeed, the penalty for the violation is death. This is so that its pages will remain unknown to the "goy" (a Talmudic term for Gentiles, meaning "cattle").

I have obtained, read, and studied the Talmud, as have some other Christians, and we have been shocked by the audacity of the rabbis as found in this book. Imagine, in the Talmud we discover that:

1. All Christians are to be killed
2. Jesus is a false prophet who corrupted Israel. He is said to be the son of a whore (Mary) who practiced bestiality with his donkey. Jesus is today burning in hot excrement in hell.
3. It is acceptable to cheat a Gentile in business.
4. The New Testament is an evil document.
5. Gentiles are animals and beasts without souls.
6. Gentiles exist only to serve the Jews.
7. The wealth of the Gentiles belongs to the Jews.
8. When a Jew walks past a Christian church or cemetery he must grab his crotch and spit three times on the ground.

This is only a small portion of the hatred and nonsense spewed out of what is supposed to be a "holy" book!

The hypocrisy of the Khazar Jews here is palpable. Not realizing that they, themselves, are Gentiles, as DNA science has shown, they cleave to a holy book, the Talmud, that is the most *anti-Gentile* of all books. Without the Talmud there would be no rabbinical Judaism, and so the Khazars simply must hold on to its monstrous doctrines to retain their Judaic religion.

Jewish Rabbis Obey the Talmud

And hold on to the Talmud they do. In 2010 and 2012 we saw prime examples of this when one of Judaism's most honored and respected rabbis, Rabbi Ovadia Yosef, was quoted in the Israeli press as proclaiming that non-Jews exist only to serve Jews. According to the Jewish Telegraphic Agency, Yosef told Israelis in his Saturday night sermon, "*Goyim* (Gentiles) were born only to serve us. Without that, they have no place in the world; only to serve the people of Israel."

Yosef compared Gentiles to donkeys and said that, as

slaves of the Jews, the loss of a Gentile would be as if one's donkey died.

It was not the first time Rabbi Yosef has said similar things, but the fact is, most Jews in Israel agree with him. Reverend Theodore Pike, a Presbyterian, laments this fact:

> "When we delve into the doctrinal foundations of modern, or Rabbinic, Judaism (the Talmud and Zohar) we find only agreement with Yosef. The rabbi speaks from lifelong immersion in this sacred literature which, to observant Jews, far surpasses the authority of the Old Testament."

Pike, in his article, then goes on to actually quote the Talmud, pointing out that, according to the rabbinical "wisdom," Gentiles (non-Jews) are like serpents, their seed is that of an animal, and that Gentiles have no souls.

Jesus Warned of the "Traditions of the Elders"

Jesus well knew of the Talmud, even though in his day it was an oral document. He spoke of the "traditions of the elders" held as sacrosanct by the Jews in a very disparaging way. He called the Pharisees (Orthodox Jews) "hypocrites," "whited sepulchers," "blind guides," and a "generation of vipers," and said that they were responsible for "all the righteous blood shed upon the earth" *(Matthew 23)*. What a ringing indictment!

Today, the rabbis and their followers continue in their pharisaic way, impressing their modern-day disciples to read, study, and obey the *halacha* (613 laws of the Talmud). The rabbis are teaching the people to hate, discriminate against, and persecute others simply because the persecuted are "Gentiles." Now we know, through DNA science evidence, that the rabbis themselves are Gentiles!

Jesus told the Jews: "If God were your father, ye would love me...ye are of your father the devil, and the lusts of your father ye will do. He was a murderer from the beginning, and abode not in the truth, because there is no truth in him..." *(John 8:42-44)*

Angered at the biting words of Jesus, "Then answered the Jews...thou hast a devil..."

The glorious work of Jesus was well summarized by the Apostle John, who wrote:

"He came unto his own, and his own received him not. But as many as received him, to them gave he power to become the sons of God, even to them that believe on his name: Which were born, not of blood, nor of the will of the flesh, nor of the will of man, but of God." (John 1:11-13)

The Jews of Jesus' day were, said the Lord, the physical blood seed of Abraham. This, of course, was before Israel was destroyed by Titus. Yet He said they were *not* the spiritual children of Abraham. If they were, they would love Him. Even though the Jews were the descendants and seed of Abraham, they were not true Jews! For Paul said that the *true Jew* would believe in Jesus Christ as Lord.

Thus, the bloodline of the Jews did the physical descendants of Abraham no spiritual good at all, for Jesus is a reader of hearts. He knew their hearts were evil, and He said so.

Who Is a Jew?

The Apostle Paul explained it by telling us who is a Jew:

"For he is not a Jew, which is one outwardly... But

*he is a Jew, which is one inwardly; and circumcision
is that of the heart, in the spirit, and not in the
letter; whose praise is not of men, but of God."
(Romans 2:28-29)*

So, the Jew is one who believes in Christ. Being a Jew is
a matter of the spirit, for a Christian is born again "in spirit and
in truth." We have two consecutive warnings in the scriptures
about "them which say they are Jews and are not..." These evil
people may physically be either Jews, actual descendants of
Abraham, or Khazars (converted Jews). But because they have
rejected the Truth which is Jesus, God exposes them as His
enemies—and ours:

*"I know thy works, and tribulation, and poverty,
(but thou art rich) and I know the blasphemy of
them which say they are Jews, and are not, but are
the synagogue of Satan." (Revelation 2:9)*

*"Behold, I will make them of the synagogue of
Satan, which say they are Jews, and are not, but do
lie; behold, I will make them to come and worship
before thy feet, and to know that I have loved thee."
(Revelation 3:9)*

Jews, Gentiles Not Equals in Israel

As this book goes to press, we have one more demonstration
of the Khazar "Jews" hatred and discrimination against non-
Jews. The head rabbi of the Israeli military, Brigadier General
Rafi Peretz, has distributed a new book which attempts to
explain a new ruling he has made. That ruling holds that non-
Jews should not have equal rights with the Jews.

The book, *Law of the Mezuzah*, by three rabbis, Alexander

Rones, Dov Berkovich, and Hananiah Shafron, is distributed to each and every military member in the Israeli Defense Forces. It says that, "the idea of giving non-Jews (that is, *Gentiles*) equal rights goes against the principles of the Torah."

Of course, this is not a new idea. In Israel today, by law, Gentiles may not own land or title to property; Christian Jews are forbidden to emigrate to Israel; and certain cemeteries are forbidden to non-Jews.

So, in effect, the Khazars of Israel, who say they are Jews and are not, are taking away their own civil rights! Is this not rank hypocrisy?

The Jews have actually never been a pure Israelite race. As John Bray, a Baptist evangelist writes:

"From the time of Abraham right on down throughout the years there were always Gentiles intermingling in this body of people known as the nation of Israel. There never was just a bloodline because there has never been such a pure race. He never chose Israel on the basis of race or blood... God's promises were made to those people who by faith kept the promises of God."

In many places in the Old Testament we read of Israel's adultery and disobedience to God. God warned the people of Israel, "I will utterly forget you. You will be utterly destroyed. You will utterly perish unless you obey my commandments."

Eventually, God withdrew His covenant (see *Hebrews 8*) and gave the people a "new and better covenant" that had faith as its principle and belief in Jesus as the only means of entering into the covenant. Whether Jew or Gentile, faith in Jesus assures the new covenant, and so, in *Romans*, it clearly states, and so *"all Israel will be saved."*

"All Israel will be saved." That means the Gentiles who believe but also the *remnant* of Jews who have faith in Jesus will be saved. But the Jews who refuse God's magnanimous offer of salvation, like the Gentiles who do not have faith, will not have everlasting life through Jesus. Thus Paul, as recorded in *Acts*, in Antioch informed the Jews:

> *"It was necessary that the word of God should first have been spoken to you: but seeing ye put it from you, and judge yourselves unworthy of everlasting life, lo, we turn to the Gentiles." (Acts 13: 46)*

Jesus is Seed of God

In this book, you have seen how God is not a racist, how he tenderly asks all people to believe in Him. Jews, Gentiles—yes, Khazars, too—have the glorious opportunity to serve God. The Khazars who call themselves "Jews" should listen closely and decide whether they will continue in their unholy Talmud or call on the Lord Jesus for salvation.

In making this momentous, life-changing decision, please take a few minutes and read these verses from the New Testament. They will inform the reader of the spiritual *seed* of God. It is the spiritual seed of God that imparts eternal life, not a person's race. Decide for yourself which seed you will sow in your life, "for whatsoever a man soweth, that shall he also reap" *(Galatians 6:7).*

> *"Now the parable is this: The seed is the word of God." (Luke 8:11)*

> *"The sower soweth the word... And these are they which are sown on good ground; such as hear the*

word, and receive it, and bring forth fruit, some thirtyfold, some sixty, and some an hundred." (Mark 4:14, 20)

"Being born again, not of corruptible seed, but of incorruptible, by the word of God, which liveth and abideth for ever." (1 Peter 1:23)

"Christ hath redeemed us from the curse of the law...that we might receive the promise of the Spirit through faith." (Galatians 3:13-14)

"It is the spirit that quickeneth (giveth life); the flesh profiteth nothing: the words that I speak unto you, they are spirit, and they are life." (John 6:63)

"For God so loved the world, that he gave his only begotten Son, that whosoever believeth in him should not perish, but have everlasting life." (John 3:16)

"And if ye be Christ's, then are ye Abraham's seed, and heirs according to the promise." (Galatians 3:29)

Jesus is the Seed, and He is Life

Christian Zionists read the Old Testament and believe that the physical seed is what counts. They do not understand that God speaks of an "incorruptible" seed, a seed that is spiritual in nature. The Zionist demotes the spiritual seed and accepts only the carnal seed. However, the New Testament adds clarity and understanding. Thus the necessity to read and heed the whole counsel of God.

When we do read and study the whole counsel of God, the Old *and* New Testament, our spirits are refreshed. We discover the glorious truth that the true and life-saving seed of Abraham is not Jewish people. It is Jesus *(Galatians 3:16)*.

Jesus is the Word of God. (John 1:1)

Jesus is Life (John 6:40)

TWELVE

America Never Recognized Israel as a "Jewish" State

How President Harry S. Truman Finally Rebelled and Said "No!" to the Jews

Did you know that then President Harry S. Truman, in 1948 refused to recognize the new fledgling state of Israel as a "Jewish" religious state? It's true, and in this chapter I present the evidence that Israel is *not* a "Jewish" state.

Once upon a time, the Zionist Jews who control America loved President Harry S. Truman. Starting the moment he was sworn in as President following the death of Franklin D. Roosevelt, Truman slavishly followed their dictates. He committed mass murders for them; he ordered the assassination of top U.S. leaders who were their enemies; he endorsed their socialist economy aims.

But most of all, working hand-in-glove with Soviet dictator Joseph Stalin, Truman literally created the nation of Israel.

Yes, Truman is the *"Father of Israel."* Under his leadership, Israel was first recognized as an independent state. Against virtually unanimous opposition within his own cabinet and in Congress, on May 14, 1948, President Truman issued a declaration recognizing Israel as a new nation in the Middle East.

Truman Given Two Million Dollar Bribe by Zionists

All Zionists were, of course, ecstatic, but the Zionist elite knew months in advance that Truman would do this. As I explain and prove in my latest investigative report, my book, *Conspiracy of the Six Pointed Star*, a Zionist powerbroker and criminal, Abraham Feinberg, had, just months before, given

Abraham Feinberg (center), Jewish spy, secretly gave President Truman (left) a bribe to recognize Israel as a state. David Ben Gurion, Israel's first Prime Minister, is on right.

the President a two-million dollar bribe— $100 bills packed in suitcases—to recognize Israel.

This bribe to Truman, confirmed by recently released FBI archives, means that Israel is today and always has been an *illegitimate* state established on the basis of a criminal act.

Israel's spies stole atomic bomb secrets from the United States.

The Truman White House was overflowing with Jewish bureaucrats, treacherous Communists, and Israel firsters with little allegiance to the U.S.A. In the Truman White House also was Harry Hopkins, a secret Soviet agent who arranged for Stalin and Russia to be given America's nuclear blueprints and materials. The fledgling nation of Israel was also given atomic bomb materials and plans.

Mass Murders, Assassinations, and Holocausts

Under orders from his Jewish superiors, Truman used nuclear bombs to massacre hundreds of thousands of Japanese in the cities of Hiroshima and Nagasaki. This in spite of the fact that the Japanese emperor and generals had already petitioned America to allow them to surrender.

Another massacre of gargantuan proportions occurred in postwar Germany when Truman, at the insistence of Jewish billionaires who were his handlers, Morgenthau and Baruch, ordered that millions of innocent German citizens—men, women, and children—be starved, frozen to death, or otherwise killed.

Truman looked the other way when many American

Harry Truman, President of the U.S.A. in his Masonic regalia.

servicemen held in German POW camps were turned over to Stalin. The Soviet monster sent the tormented American servicemen to torturous Soviet gulags where they eventually died of overwork and starvation.

Implementing what was called the *Morgenthau Plan*, the psychopath President and his cohort, Stalin, had millions of Germans rounded up and taken to the same concentration camps previously run by the Nazis. In some of these camps (see the book, *An Eye for An Eye*, by Jewish newsman John Sack), believe it or not, inhuman Jewish guards and Camp Commandants raped and tortured the German women and children. The heads of little babies were smashed against walls, and male prisoners were often beaten to death.

China was turned over to the ruthless Communist, Mao Tse Tung, by Truman. This was a significant blow to Asia and has had the most horrific reverberations for America ever since. It turns out that the Jews were responsible for this atrocity as well. In my book, *Conspiracy of the Six-Pointed Star*, I name the two Jews, Sidney Shapiro and Irving Epstein, who were in charge of Mao Tse Tung's banking and finance and the media of Red China.

Truman and his Jewish bosses refused to allow General MacArthur to vigorously prosecute the war that had broken out in Korea. When the veteran General objected to Truman's coddling the Communist invaders, he was fired by the cocky President.

Shocker!—Israel Is Not A Jewish State

While President Truman, for the most part, meticulously followed the marching orders dictated to him by his Zionist overlords, he privately chafed about his subordinate status. He despised the Jews' smug, superior attitudes and resented the fact that they had bribed him to recognize Israel.

Interestingly, Truman finally rebelled in what appears to have been a small but was actually a very significant way. When the declaration to recognize Israel was brought to him for his signature, it first read: *"...the new Jewish State of Israel."* Truman took his pen and lined through the words "new Jewish." This meant that the U. S. recognized *not* a *"new Jewish State"*—a religious and racial designation—but instead simply a "State."

To this day, the Zionists insist theirs is a "Jewish" State. In other words, a Jewish religious theocracy. But this is not so. Israel was recognized by President Truman and the U.S. as a *secular* State, not as a Jewish religious theocracy. This has tremendous significance for the Palestinians. Today, the Palestinians are unfairly treated as non-citizens in Israel. They are allowed neither to vote or to own property, as the Jews spout the fiction that Israel was founded as a Jewish State and those of other races and religions do not belong.

Truman's Appraisal of Jews

Years after Truman's death, found in his files was this entry dated July 21, 1947 from the *President's Personal Diary:*

> "The Jews, I find are very selfish...when they
> have power, physical or political, neither Hitler

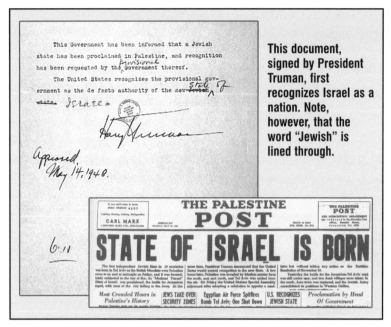

This document, signed by President Truman, first recognizes Israel as a nation. Note, however, that the word "Jewish" is lined through.

nor Stalin has anything on them for cruelty or mistreatment to the underdog."

Because of this entry in his *Personal Diary*, many of the Jewish elite have belatedly branded Harry S. Truman an "anti-Semite." Which goes to show that to the Jews, no matter how slavishly one serves the cause of Israel and Zionism, even a private opinion written in one's personal papers leaves that person vulnerable to unfair, smear charges of anti-Semitism.

Still, no one can accurately say that President Harry Truman did not fully understand the unpatriotic sentiments and attitudes of the Jews who reside in America. After his retirement, in 1956, Truman confided in an interview his knowledge that American Jews were disloyal to the U.S. He stated: *"When a Jew born and living in America talks to his Jewish companions about 'our government,' he means the government of Israel."*

THIRTEEN

Are You a True Christian? Can You Pass This Qualifying Test?

Jewish Witchcraft, Money, Sex and The Parable of the Seed

"Ye serpents, ye generation of vipers, how can
ye escape the damnation of hell."
                                    —*Matthew 23:33*

Is there a test, or standard, we can apply to identify who is a true Christian? Can you and I distinguish between a man or woman who is a true Christian and one who is a Judaizer counterfeit "Christian?" Are there also people who pretend or think they are "Christian" but actually are Talmudic worshippers of either sex or filthy lucre (money)?

A vast majority of America's 300 million residents profess to be of the Christian faith. Thousands of churches dot the American landscape and each has a pastor or minister who is said to be a "Christian." But are all these people *really* of Christ Jesus? Are all, or even most, of the men (and women) who stand behind pulpits in churches big and small really ministers of the Christian Gospel? Is *Jesus Christ* their Lord and Savior?

1,001 Jesuses

Some time ago, I recorded a special message entitled, *1,001 Jesuses*. I explained how some who claim to be Christian believe in a Jesus who never performed any miracles. Others confess a Jesus who is not God but was a great prophet, a wandering sage, or one of a long line of holy men. Some New Agers say that Jesus was a reincarnated Egyptian high priest, or an Ascended Master from an unseen dimension. Freemasons secretly hail Jesus as a representative of the Grand Architect of the Universe, but deny He is truly God.

Mormons (LDS) teach of a Jesus who had and has many wives and is a polygamist. He is also said to be a man who earned his godhood. Their doctrine holds that Jesus is one of many "gods" and is god only of this one planet, earth. Jehovah's Witnesses claim that Jesus is yet another name for Michael the Archangel. They say he is not God.

What a blooming buzz of confusion we find when we investigate the proliferation of Jesuses out there in human *la la* land. Surely, Satan is the author of confusion.

Beware "Another Jesus" and "Another Gospel"

My investigation shows that few of the multitudes who proclaim themselves "Christian" are worshippers of the *real Jesus*. Most have some strange concoction in their head of the particular "Jesus" whom they boast is their god or role model. But close examination often proves that their "Jesus" is quite a different entity than the one described in the sacred scriptures. Most people, in fact, are followers, or pretend to be followers, of a *counterfeit Jesus*, a Christ figure they have made up and constructed from their own vain imagination.

How very true it is that the Bible cautions against unholy worship of "another Jesus" and adherence to *"another Gospel."* As Paul warns in *2 Corinthians 11:3-4:*

> *"But I fear, lest by any means, as the serpent beguiled Eve through his subtilty, so your minds should be corrupted from the simplicity that is in Christ.*
>
> *For if he that cometh preacheth another Jesus, whom we have not preached, or if ye receive another spirit, which ye have not received, or another gospel, which ye have not accepted, ye might well bear with him."*

Witchcraft is Rebellion Against God

What would lead a man or woman to believe in "another Jesus" and to heed "another Gospel?" Invariably, I find that such people are rebels against God, no matter how much they feign to be holy and pious. Their life is based on deceit and selfishness, and rebellion (animosity) against the Truth inevitably follows.

Rebellion against God, the scriptures say, is witchcraft. These people, then, are witches. Though they may not boil frogs in cauldrons, do not cast spells, and do not offer magic potions, nevertheless, their lives are embroiled in heresy and witchcraft.

How can we know whether a person is a rebellious witch? How can we discover that their "Jesus" is bogus and a self-made creation—a figment of their own poisoned mind? Thankfully, the Bible offers us a simple test. Simple, yes, but also profound. I have often employed this test to startling effect.

Here is the test: Ask the self-professed "Christian" if he or she can tell you what is the *seed* of God?

The Parable of the Seed

Now Jesus taught the *Parable of the Seed* (also called the Parable of the Sower), and this teaching is recorded in three different Gospels, Matthew, Mark, and Luke. In *Mark 4*, Christ was asked by his disciples to explain this parable. In response, Jesus said something so vital and thrilling, so incredibly important it boggles the mind and causes one's heart to race.

Jesus first told his disciples that they and all others who believe in Him are of the kingdom of God. As His children, they are given discernment to understand this parable and to *"know the mystery of the kingdom of God."* But, said Christ, those who are outside, who are not of the kingdom, will not understand this Parable of the Seed. Indeed, he emphasized, those outside His fold cannot know the mystery of the kingdom of God. If a person were to understand, he would be converted and his sins forgiven.

We read in *Mark 4:11-12*:

"And he said unto them, Unto you it is given to know the mystery of the kingdom of God: but unto them that are without, all these things are done in parables:

That seeing they may see, and not perceive; and

*hearing they may hear, and not understand; lest at
any time they should be converted, and their sins
should be forgiven them."*

Wow! What an amazing teaching. But Jesus wasn't
finished. He then told His disciples that if they understood this
one parable, that of the Seed, they would understand *all* His
parables. But if they did not understand the Parable of the
Seed, they would *not* understand *any* of His parables.

I reiterate: If a person understands Christ's Parable of the
Seed, he will (1) Be converted and his sins forgiven; (2) Know
the mystery of God; and (3) Understand all of Jesus' parables,
as taught in the Gospels.

Conversely, if a person does not understand the Parable of
the Seed: (1) He will remain unconverted and his sins will *not*
be forgiven; (2) He will *not* know the Mystery of God; and (3)
He will *not* understand any of Jesus' parables.

Obviously, this is the most important and essential of all
Jesus' parables. If a person does not possess this knowledge,
he or she is *not* a Christian—is *not* of Christ Jesus—but rather
is in bondage to Satan.

Thus, any person who cannot accurately respond to the
question, "What is the seed?" is not a true Christian. He may
say he is, and he may think he is a Christian, but he is not. We
say this by the authority of the Word of the only One who can
forgive sins and save souls: Jesus Christ.

What the Seed is, and is Not

So, given its central role in salvation and forgiveness, what (or
who) is the seed of God? Do *you* know? First, let us examine
three false answers to this question. Then, lastly, we will
provide the *scriptural* answer to the all-important question,
who or *what* is the seed?

False Answer No. 1—The Seed is Money

Word of Faith teachers like Kenneth Copeland, Paul Crouch, Creflo Dollar, Joyce Meyer, Benny Hinn, and Paula White fail the test because their answer is that the "seed" is the money that a person gives. They preach the "Seed Faith" message, and tens of millions of people worldwide believe their testimony. Give money to these televangelists, to your church, or to ministries of God, and God will bless you. Give to get, that is their message. Plant your seed and prosper. God will make you rich. Want a romantic mate, a high paying job, a big bank account, a Mercedes car, a yacht, a mansion? Then, plant your seed of money.

The seed, according to these deceived multitudes, is money. This is their Gospel—a Prosperity Gospel of material rewards right here on earth. Filthy lucre.

By their Seed Faith Gospel ye shall know them, for the seed is not money. Indeed, Jesus, in explaining the Parable of the Seed to his disciples, actually told them that it is the lure of money that *prevents* the seed from taking hold and growing. He who seeks after money and worldly things, says Christ, *"Are they which are sown among thorns!"*

> *"And the cares of this world, and the deceitfulness of riches, and the lust of other things entering in, choke the word, and it becometh unfruitful."*

The prosperity, or "Seed Faith," preachers foolishly—or perhaps calculatingly—often call theirs the "Word of Faith" Gospel. But Jesus Himself testified that what they teach and practice actually *chokes* the Word and it becomes unfruitful.

Ah yes, as Paul cautioned the young Timothy: *"The love of money is the root of all evil."*

And so we know that all those who teach and profess the

"Seed Faith" money/prosperity Gospel are not true Christians. They can speak in tongues, dance in the aisles of their churches, and hold up their hands all they want. They can dissolve in "holy laughter," it won't make a difference at all. Their name will *not* be found written in the book of life. Jesus said so—if they do not understand the Parable of the Seed, they are not converted and their sins are unforgiven. They have not been pressed into the Kingdom and so the riches of this world—for which they so ardently lust and hunger—shall be their only reward. Until, that is, Satan takes them to his fiery abode to live forever with he and his dark angels.

False Answer No. 2—The Seed is the Jewish Race

There is yet another large segment of establishment Christianity who, when asked to explain the Seed, will respond: *"The seed is made up of all the Jews. They are God's Chosen People. The Jews are the seed of Abraham."* This we might well call the "Seed Race" doctrine.

These pseudo-Christians, whom we may correctly call "Judaizers," "Zionists," or "Judaic-Christians," are, like the Word of Faith crowd, also lustfully into a form, or variant, of Prosperity Gospel. The Jews, they say, are the seed and if a Christian blesses the Jew (and Israel) with money and material things (or with guns, tanks, bombs, etc.), then God will bless the giver. Give to get, same as Copeland, Crouch and others.

Sadly, once again we discover that these evangelical Judaic-Christians radically miss the mark. To them, the seed is a matter of blood and race. Flesh, they fervently teach, is of the utmost importance—specifically the flesh of the Jews. In their theology, Abraham's heirs, his physical "seed" are put on a pedestal and adored—the Jews are elevated supernaturally above Gentiles and became a superior god-race, cream of the earth.

Now the Jews no doubt find this "Seed Race" teaching of the Judaizer evangelicals both convenient and flattering. It is no wonder, then, that the government of Israel throws the nation's doors open to Judaizer tour groups and other pro-Zionist visitors who preach this unholy doctrine. Untold millions of donated dollars in aid money flood in to Israel from these deluded worshippers and adorers of the physical seed of Abraham.

The Judaizers also are the backbone of political support for Israel in the United States. Indeed, the many wars fought by American forces in Iraq, Afghanistan, Pakistan and elsewhere are supported by the evangelical masses who are convinced America is doing God's will in defending a militant Israel from the Arab and Moslem "hordes."

As a result, Israel has over the years received hundreds of billions in foreign aid and armaments paid for by U.S. taxpayers. Corrupt American politicians even covertly arranged for Israel to receive nuclear bombs, with which they now threaten their neighbors.

Jesus Rejected the "Seed Race" Doctrine

Jesus, in the Gospel of Matthew, came up against this doctrine of Jewish supremacism.

When the Jews arrogantly and pridefully insisted to Jesus that they were the heirs and seed of Abraham and claimed that Abraham was their father, Jesus did not hesitate to refute their claim! Yes, He retorted, I know you are Abraham's seed—in other words, of the physical lineage of Abraham through the flesh. But, Jesus said, your real father is the devil!

"Ye serpents, ye generation of vipers," He angrily snapped at the Jewish hypocrites, "how can ye escape the damnation of hell" *(Matthew 23:33)?*

Unless they repented of their arrogant pride and their other sins, the Jews, Jesus taught, were hell-bound. So much for the Judaizers' racial doctrine of the seed.

Catholics Join Evangelists in Seed Race Apostasy

Interestingly, in its *New Catholic Cathechism*, promulgated by the former Pope, John Paul II, a variant of this same doctrine which exalts the Jews as our "elder brothers" is found. The evangelicals—mostly Baptists and Pentecostals—now find common ground on this matter with Roman Catholics.

Rebuilding the Temple—Yet Another Heresy

Confirming just how confused and chaotic is the unscriptural theology of the Judaizers, we also discover that the rabbis' outlandish proposal for an earthly kingdom of the Jews is heavily promoted today by the evangelical Judaizers. The hearts desire of the Judaic Christian is to give money and enthusiastic political support to the Jewish rabbis who seek to rebuild the Temple in Jerusalem.

You mean the very Temple that Jesus, in the Gospel of Matthew prophesied would be thrown down, stone upon stone? Yes, the very Temple that Jesus commanded be destroyed. The Judaic Christians work and strive to rebuild it, in defiance of Jesus' edict. Such is the theology of those who contend that the physical, or fleshly, "seed of Abraham" takes center stage in the Kingdom of God.

"Judaic" Christians are not True Christians

But the *Seed* of God, as Jesus noted, is not of fleshly, DNA material. Nor does a Temple made with human hands have anything to do with the seed of which Jesus spoke in His Parable of the Seed. Thus, we can know that the Judaic Christians, who preach the centrality of the fleshly, or physical, seed of Abraham, are *not* true Christians. Though they beat their breasts and proclaim their love of the Jews and of Israel, they are not Christians. They know not the Mystery of God. They have no understanding of the Parable of the Seed nor of any parable of Jesus. Their sins are not forgiven and they are not converted. They are not citizens of the Kingdom of God. Indeed, many of these Judaizer disciples of a physical Israel actually believe the Kingdom is of the Jews!

The Judaizers do not realize they have fallen into witchcraft and rebellion against God. They best heed the admonition of Paul who, seeing that the people of Galatia were teaching a similar doctrine, declared:

> *"O foolish Galatians, who hath bewitched you, that ye should not obey the truth, before whose eyes Jesus Christ hath been evidently set forth, crucified among you?"*

False Answer No. 3—The Seed is Sexual in Nature

The Freemasons are, in essence, a sex cult. Thus it is that in its higher, esoteric teachings, initiates of the Masonic Lodge understand the seed as mystically being the "elixir of life," the substance exuded from sexual intercourse. The holy sex ritual practiced in the temples of Egypt, Persia, Babylon, Rome, and Greece is a foundation of Masonic religion and is symbolically, though subtly, represented in the Masonic Lodge's 33 ritual ceremonies. Theirs is a depraved philosophy which includes the teaching that man is a much reincarnated being, and that man may, through initiation and self-will, aspire to and achieve divinity.

Through the wisdom of the ancient Jews, Egyptians and other pagans, the Mason believes that "serpent power," a Luciferian energy force, can be wielded by the higher initiate. The seed, as far as Freemasonry is concerned, is the spiritual product of a man earning his divinity and otherworldly rewards through good works and gnosis. For the Mason, the seed, in reality, is demonic possession.

The doctrines of Freemasonry—and especially the "Seed Sex" doctrines—are obviously diametrically opposed to those of Christianity. Even though a Mason may profess that he is a Christian, the teachings of the Lodge attest otherwise. The Mason understands neither the Parable of the Seed nor the Mystery of God.

So the Freemason is not a true Christian. Neither is the Word of Faith believer or the Judaic Christian.

Jesus Explains the Parable of the Seed

What, then, is the explanation of the seed? What is the meaning of the Parable of the Seed? Do you, dear reader, understand its significance? Are you truly a Christian? Can you pass the test of true Christianity? What is your understanding of the Parable of the Seed?

Listen closely to Jesus, as he teaches the profound doctrine of the seed:

> *"Now the parable is this: The seed is the word of God." (Luke 8:11)*

What marvelous simplicity! Do you understand? Do you get it? *John 1* tells us that Jesus *is* the Word of God; He is Emmanuel, God with us. In other scriptures we see that Jesus is the One who came into the world to destroy the works of the Devil, to mend the brokenhearted, to set the captives free, to save the lost, to give men new life in Him, to forgive men of their transgressions and make them whole. Jesus, the Word, was with God from the beginning and is God. He framed the heavens, set the stars in place, and created the earth.

Only the spiritual can understand this parable. The seed is the Word; thus, the seed is Jesus, the Word, planted in the heart of a regenerated man or woman. He is the way, the life, the truth. If a man has this seed planted in him, he will produce fruit. He will know the Mystery of God, for Jesus, the Apostle Paul revealed, is the "mystery of godliness."

As Paul also declared, *"Christ in you, the hope of glory!"* In other words, the seed in you, if you are a true Christian, is Jesus Himself!

The Seed is Not the Many People of Physical Israel

Paul went to great lengths to make sure that true Christians are not deceived by false doctrine, especially that spread by those who propagate *"Jewish fables"* regarding the seed. Paul even stressed that the seed is *one*, that is, Jesus, and is not the many of the Jewish nation:

> *"Now to Abraham and his seed were the promises made. He (God) saith not, And to seeds, as of many, but as of one, And to thy seed, which is Christ."*
> *(Galatians 3:16)*

What beauty is found in this passage! Abraham was given a promise by God of an eternal inheritance, of a heavenly City where Almighty God abides on the throne. The patriarch was told by God that these blessings would come through "thy seed." And *who* is "thy seed," the seed of Abraham? Paul explains that this seed is not the "many" who physically make up the temporal nation of Israel. Instead, the seed is *one*—that is, Jesus Christ.

The blessing and promise is Jesus Christ, and Abraham received that blessing and promise. What greater gift can a man receive than Christ Jesus?

The Seed are the Children of God by Faith in Jesus Christ

Moreover, all who are Christ's—who have faith in Him—are of the seed, which is Christ's spirit: *"For ye are all the children of God by faith in Jesus Christ" (Galatians 3:26).* This means Jews and Gentiles alike—if they know Christ as Lord and Savior, they are His seed and, by supernatural extension, are also the seed of Abraham:

> *"And if ye be Christ's, then are ye Abraham's seed, and heirs according to the promise." (Galatians 3:29)*

I challenge you: Ask a Judaizer Christian—a pro-Israel nationalist evangelical who has been deceived and believes in the "Jews are God's Chosen People" doctrine, if Christian Gentiles are Abraham's seed. Doubtless, he will respond, *"No, a Gentile cannot be Abraham's seed, only Jews can be. It's a matter of race, not faith"* Next, read *Galatians 3:29* to him and he'll exit the scene pronto. The Judaizer wants no part of this scripture. He flatly doesn't understand it.

The Doctrine of Christ: The Blessed Hope of Glory

No, the seed is not money, it is not flesh or race. It certainly is not the product of a sexual rite, as the Masons allege.

The seed is veritably the Word of God; the seed is Jesus Christ in a born again person's heart. That is the doctrine of Christ, the hope of every true Christian. Thus we read in *1 Peter 1:18-25*:

> *"Forasmuch as ye know that ye were not redeemed with corruptible things, as silver and gold, from your vain conversation received by tradition from your fathers;*

But with the precious blood of Christ, as of a lamb without blemish and without spot:

Who verily was foreordained before the foundation of the world, but was manifest in these last times for you,

Who by him do believe in God, that raised him up from the dead, and gave him glory; that your faith and hope might be in God.

Seeing ye have purified your souls in obeying the truth through the Spirit unto unfeigned love of the brethren, see that ye love one another with a pure heart fervently:

Being born again, not of corruptible seed, but of incorruptible, by the word of God, which liveth and abideth for ever.

For all flesh is as grass, and all the glory of man as the flower of grass. The grass withereth, and the flower thereof falleth away:

But the word of the Lord endureth for ever. And this is the word which by the gospel is preached unto you."

Are you, dear friend of truth, born again of incorruptible seed? Do you know Jesus Christ as Lord and Saviour? Are you saved by the grace of God, rather than by race? If so, you are an eternal creature, which, quickened by the Word of God, shall *"liveth and abideth forever."*

FOURTEEN

The Holy Scriptures Make Clear that Christians, Not Jews, Are to be Blessed and Shall Possess the Land

Who Has the Blessing?

"Abraham is the father of us all," says Paul in Galatians. How did this man achieve such a wonderful distinction? The scriptures tell us he obeyed God, but that was not why Abraham was so blessed. He *"believed* and it was accounted to him for righteousness," we are told.

Abraham had faith. He believed. What a great example for you and me. Let's take a look at Abraham's classic story.

"Now the Lord said unto Abram, Get thee out of thy country, and from thy kindred, and from thy father's house, unto a land that I will show thee...

And I will bless them that bless thee, and curse him that curse thee: and in thee shall all families of the earth be blessed..." (Genesis 12).

147

And so, Abraham left Ur, his residence in Chaldea, and traveled to the land that God was to show him.

Who Shall Possess the Land?

"and the Lord said unto Abraham... Lift up now thine eyes and look from the place where thou art northward, and southward, and eastward, and westward.

For all the land which thou seest, to thee will I give it, and to thy Seed forever..." (Genesis 13)

So we see that Abraham followed God's leading and was shown a great land that would become the possession of his seed.

Almost every day it seems, I receive a critical letter or email from a sincere—but often scripturally illiterate person who tries to convince me that if I bless the *Jews*, God will bless me; but if I don't, God will curse me. They claim this is according to the scriptures.

Now I want to be nice to such misguided folks, so I often write them back and ask them to please cite the exact Bible verse they use as their authority to say I must *bless* the Jews or be cursed. I rarely hear back from them. Why? Well because what they say is *not found* anywhere in the Bible.

What the Bible *does* say, in *Genesis 12*, is that if a person *blesses Abraham*, God will bless, and whoever *curses Abraham*, God will curse.

The passage that says this is *Genesis 12:3* which states:

"And I will bless them that bless <u>thee</u>, and curse him that curseth thee: and in thee shall all families of the earth be blessed."

Notice please, that the blessing or curse refers specifically to Abraham, not to the "Jews." There were no Jews in those days!

In fact, the word "Jew" is not found anywhere in the book of Genesis, and nowhere in the entire Bible is there a warning from God that God will bless us if we bless the Jews.

(Note: In the book of *Acts* we do find that an offering was taken by the saints for the *Christian Church* at Jerusalem because of economic hardship in that city. The offering went to Christians, not to unsaved Jews!)

So to those letter writers who demand that I especially bless the "Jews," you have no Scripture to stand on. In fact, you are abusing and misusing God's Word and should stop this outrage immediately.

Christian Zionists Believe Jewish Fables

Now, it's bad enough that there are so many of these Judaizers and pro-Zionists Christians abusing *Genesis 12*, but often they don't care. Some go on to inform me that the blessings of Abraham are reserved only for the Jews and that Christians are excluded from being blessed! They say that God especially loves the "Jews" over all other peoples. And they claim that this blessing goes to the Jews because they alone are the "seed of Abraham."

I forgive these misguided souls for their heresies but I believe it incumbent on me to correct the "Jewish fables" they are disseminating far and wide.

First, I must stress once again that these claims of Jewish exclusiveness have absolutely *no* scriptural basis. Unlike the biblically illiterate people who erroneously claim it is the "Jews" who must receive this blessing but cannot find this anywhere in the scriptures, I am able to cite the exact verses that tell us who is Abraham's seed and thus have both the *promise* and the *blessing*. In *Galatians 3:7-29* we read:

> *"Know ye therefore that they which are of faith, the same are the children of Abraham...*
>
> *That the blessing of Abraham might come on the Gentiles through Jesus Christ; that we might receive the promise of the Spirit through faith...*
>
> *Now to Abraham and his seed were the promises made. He saith not, And to seeds, as of many; but as of one, And to thy seed, which is Christ.*
>
> *There is neither Jew nor Greek, there is neither bond nor free, there is neither male nor female: for ye are all one in Christ Jesus...*
>
> *And if ye be Christ's, then are ye Abraham's seed, and heirs according to the promise."*

Oh what a marvelous God we serve who clears out all the spidery cobwebs of confusion spun by Satan and his human disciples. The scriptures say—and this is irrefutable—that *you are not Abraham's seed because you are a Jew, but because you have Jesus as Lord and Savior.*

So, allow me please to enlighten the Judaizers and Zionists as to the clarity and perfection of God's Word. The scriptures tell us that Christians (Jew *or* Gentile, race is irrelevant) are the very *seed* of Abraham and are *heir to the promises* God gave Abraham. Therefore:

> *Whoever blesses Christians will be blessed by God and whoever curses Christians will be cursed by God.*

Ah yes, this is far different than the fabrications which the Jews have convinced so many confused, biblically illiterate Christians. These sincere folks took it for granted that in referring to the "seed" of Abraham the Bible was speaking of the *physical seed*, or bloodline of Abraham. That would be the people who say they are "Jews" now, wouldn't it?

But, *uh oh*, these are the people that John the Baptist and Jesus both identified as *"vipers."* Jesus said to the "Jews"— *"ye are of your father the devil, and his works ye will do."*

Dear Friends, think...think: would God instruct us to bless the very people that He called "vipers;" and that he identified as being children of the devil?!

To make matters worse, we discover that the new DNA science proves that these people, who say they are Jews and are not, are actually *Khazars!* So these are *not* the Jews of Jesus' day at all. This is confusing, isn't it?

But remember, God is not the author of confusion. His Word provides us clear and convincing answers. That is why the Holy Bible actually contains its very own dictionary. That's right, as Gail Riplinger explains in her excellent book, *The Language of the King James Bible*, the Authorized King James Version of the Bible contains its own built-in dictionary.

Thus, God's word first mentions the "seed" of Abraham in *Genesis*; then, God explains who the seed are—He defines the word "seed" in several other key places, including in *Galatians 3*. It is extremely important we always consult the *"whole counsel"* of God, as this prime example attests.

The Land is Given to the Seed of Abraham

Finally, our confused and biblically mixed-up friends in the Judaizer and pro-Zionist camp want us to accept that God has given the "Jews" the land of Greater Israel for a permanent possession. But alas, they are unable to point to even one verse that proves this falsehood. Not one.

In contrast, we discover, in *Genesis 13*, that it is *the seed of Abraham* that is promised the land that Abraham saw. God told Abraham: "To thee will I give it and to thy seed."

I have already demonstrated that the "seed" is not the "Jews" as a race or nation. The seed of Abraham are those who have faith in and are of Jesus. They are called out of all nations on earth, and this is why God promised Abraham that (1) He would become the "father of many nations;" and (2) "In thee (Abraham) shall all families of the earth be blessed."

God Keeps Promises

Indeed, God kept these promises. The seed of Abraham is Jesus and those who believe in Him. In fact, through this "seed," the whole world has come to know the magnificent Gospel of the Kingdom. Through Jesus and the evangelism (the Great Commission) of Abraham's seed, the Christians, all the world is blessed! Can this be refuted?

As Christians are the seed of Abraham, then it is *they*, not the "Jews," who will possess the land, for the scriptures say that it is the seed who will possess it. The passages in *Genesis 13* do not mention the Jews. No, only the seed, are referred to, and according to *Galatians 3:29*, the seed are those who have faith in Christ Jesus.

Not only will Christians, the seed, possess the limited portion of earth known as Israel, they shall inherit and reign *over all the earth*:

> *"And he that overcometh, and keepeth my works unto the end, to him will I give power over the nations. And he shall rule them with a rod of iron..." (Revelation 2:26)*

DNA SCIENCE AND THE JEWISH BLOODLINE ○ 153

All the World is Blessed by Jesus

Now Abraham's seed, the Bible says, will bless "all families of the earth." How is this done? By the preaching of the Gospel of the Kingdom! Yes, by telling a person how he can receive Jesus as His personal Savior, we bless that person immensely and enrich his or her life greatly.

Do the Jews bless people? Do Khazars? Of course not. Through their religion, they actually bring bondage and misery into people's lives.

Christian Zionists rarely evangelize the Jews. Many believe the Jews have their own covenant with God. So, no blessing is possible.

But when the Judaizers and Zionists speak of "blessing the Jews" they usually mean they want us to support the Jews in Israel in stealing more and more land from the Palestinians, Lebanese, and other Arabs.

Blessing the Jews, they say, also means arming the Jews to the teeth with military aircraft, bombs, tanks, and other supplies so that Israel can be the "big dog" militarily in the Middle East.

The Judaizers and Zionists also want us to continually send billions and billions of U.S. taxpayer dollars to Israel even though Israel is a socialist, racist nation, a religious theocracy that discriminates against Christians and people who are not Jews.

Never—I repeat—Never have I ever heard a Judaizer or Zionist "Christian" teach that the best way to "bless the Jews" is to give them Jesus! How sick is that? The Judaizers and Zionists care little about the *souls* of the lost and unsaved Jews. Most are not at all interested in witnessing to the Jews. In fact, many Judaizers and Zionists refuse to evangelize, explaining they do not want to "offend" the Jews.

In effect, the Judaizers and Zionists refuse to carry out the Great Commission of Christ Jesus. They are obviously confused over the definition of the word "blessing."

Do You Really Want to Bless the Jews?

If you and I want to "bless the Jews," the best way to do so is not to endorse Israel's brutal mistreatment of Palestinians and Arabs. We have not blessed the Jews by making their tiny nation, Israel, the world's *fourth* most powerful military power, complete with nuclear bombs and missile-carrying nuclear submarines, nor do we do God's work by filling the coffers of socialist Israel annually with billions of our foreign aid money so Jewish billionaires can build skyscrapers and Mediterranean beach hotels and resorts.

The best way—the only lasting way—you and I can bless Israel and the Jews is to preach the Kingdom of God to them.

While nearby Palestinians live in poverty and squalor, Israeli citizens enjoy a luxurious life on the Mediterranean.

Tell them the blunt truth, as did Jesus—that they are headed to hell because they despise and hate Christ. But God loves them and will forgive them if they repent.

The Jews' Conspiracy Against God Fails

As I have explained, those who pridefully say they have Abraham as their Father and who refuse to worship Jesus Christ as Lord and Savior are rebels against God. Those who say they are Jews and are not are the *Synagogue of Satan (Revelation 2:9* and *3:9)*. New DNA science research proves conclusively that almost all the people who today say they are Jews are not Jews at all. They are Khazarian. But, whether Khazarian or Jew, they shall be judged, and if they refuse to accept Christ Jesus they shall receive their just punishment in everlasting hell. This is true also for Gentiles who reject Christ and refuse to serve Him.

The Synagogue of Satan, though its people have plotted and schemed for centuries in a grand conspiracy to destroy Christ and His Church, shall fail. As we read in *Revelation 11:15*:

> *"And the seventh angel sounded; and there were great voices in heaven, saying, The kingdoms of this world are become the kingdoms of our Lord, and of his Christ; and he shall reign for ever and ever."*

FIFTEEN

Old Testament Prophets Looked Not for an Earthly Jerusalem

Jews and Judaizers Have Made an Idol of the Nation of Israel

Abraham, say the scriptures, looked not for a temple and a city built by human hands, but toward a heavenly city built by God. As the scriptures put it, Abraham's desire was for a city promised Him by God: *"...a city which hath foundations whose builder and maker is God..." (Hebrews 11:10)*

Abraham and all the Old Testament prophets considered themselves strangers and pilgrims on earth. They sought instead a *"better country, that is, a heavenly: wherefore God... hath prepared for them a city." (Hebrews 11:13-16)*

Today, Zionist Jews (Khazars) and evangelical Judaizers have exalted the earthly city of Jerusalem. It has become an idol. They venerate the city and blasphemously call it "holy." But Abraham would not agree. He looked not to an earthly city, but to a heavenly. As Paul expressed it, *"For here we have no continuing city, but we seek one to come" (Hebrews 13:14).*

Judaizers are intent on helping today's aggressively radical Zionist Jews and Israel militarily oppress the Palestinians and "take back the land." In reality, God promised the land to Abraham's seed—men and women of any and all races and nations who have faith in Christ Jesus—and *not* to either Christ-rejecting Jews *or* to Arab Moslems. Christians are the seed and *they* are to inherit *all* things *(Galatians 3:29).*

Paul: "Here We Have No Continuing City"

But Christians, though heirs of all, look not to this earthly City and Kingdom. Sadly, ignorant pseudo-Christian Judaizers are helping the earthly Jews seize every bit of Mid-East dirt they can to set up a powerful Jewish State. The Zionists desire a carnal kingdom right here on earth, but as Jesus told Pilate, "My kingdom is not of this world." God's people, in contrast, look toward heaven for redemption, and fully understand that, as Paul wrote, here on earth *"we have no continuing city..."*

Thus, the Bible clearly teaches that Christian believers, God's Chosen People, chosen out of all earthly races and nations, have *no continuing citizenship in any nation on earth*, nor are they tied to earthly Jerusalem or to any other city on earth. As Paul stated, Christians are citizens of *heavenly Jerusalem,* the Holy City of God. This alone is the abode of Abraham's seed, Christ's own.

Jesus prophesied that earthly Jerusalem and Israel would remain "desolate" until he returns. *(Matthew 23:37-39)* Desolate means devoid of value, worthless from a spiritual perspective.

Jesus: "I am Not of This World"

Jesus well knew that the Jews were craven materialists and that in their ungodly teachings—common in today's Judaism—they greedily declare that, eventually, the Jewish Kingdom will dominate planet earth. When that occurs, the Jews believe, all the wealth of the Gentiles (i.e. the *goyim—cattle*) would be theirs. Their mania for worldly power and riches clearly stamps the Jews as Satan's deluded disciples. Therefore, Christ flatly told the Jews:

> *Ye neither know me, nor my Father...I go my way, and ye shall seek me, and shall die in your sins: Whither I go, Ye cannot come...Ye are from beneath: I am from above: ye are of this world: I am not of this world.*

> *I said therefore unto you, that ye shall die in your sins: for if ye believe not that I am he, ye shall die in your sins." (John 8: 19-24)*

Doing God's Work by Assisting Satan?

I have met many deceived Christians who, ignorant of the scriptures, but believing their evangelical teachers, sincerely believe they are doing God's work by helping the Jews (including the Khazar Jews, who are the majority of the world's Jews) build an earthly (i.e. a *worldly*) kingdom. They often consider Zionism *the* most important work a Christian can do, and they imagine that God will bless them for assisting the Jews to seize and hold Palestinian lands. They are so carnally deceived they actually believe God will give them material blessings if they help Israel and the Jews succeed in their satanic earthly goals. This is a very deceptive form of *"prosperity gospel."*

Zionist Christians Hope for Material Rewards

Having fallen for the "prosperity gospel" lie, many Judaizers/ Zionist "Christians" are actually giving money to Orthodox Jewish rabbis and radicals to help them rebuild the Temple in Jerusalem! This even though the Apostle Paul said that the Son of Perdition, the beast 666, will use this unholy place, a rebuilt Temple, to commit the sacrilege of declaring himself above God *(2 Thessalonians 2)*.

Earthly Jerusalem is "Sodom and Egypt"

Indeed, earthly Jerusalem is identified in prophetic scriptures not as a holy place but as a wicked and vile city. God even calls it spiritual *"Sodom and Egypt" (Revelation 11:8-9)*. The Apostle Paul wrote that earthly Jerusalem and its people are "in bondage" to Satan. Moreover, Paul warned that Jews who continue under the old covenant are spiritually the descendents of Agar, the bondwoman (slave) and her son, Ishmael *(Galatians 4:21-31)*.

Paul emphasized that *Christians* are free and are citizens of the heavenly Jerusalem that is above. Thus, Christian believers are the heritage and seed of Sarah's son, Isaac, while Jews who cling to the decayed and now nonexistent, old covenant are spiritually kin to Agar, the slave woman and her son, Ishmael.

> *"For this Agar...answereth (corresponds) to Jerusalem which now is and is in bondage with her children. But Jerusalem which is above is free... Now we, brethren, as Isaac was, are the children of promise... So, then, brethren, we are not children of the bondwoman, but of the free." (Galatians 4:21-31)*

How many pastors have you ever heard preach this truth that the Jews, and Jerusalem in the Middle East, are the spiritual descendants of the bondwoman, Agar, and her son, Ishmael? And consider, too, that the bondwoman Agar, and her son were cast OUT into the desert!

Just so, Paul explains that Jews who reject Christ are "cast out" of the Kingdom of God: *"...For the son of the bondwoman shall not be heir with the son of the freewoman" (Galatians 4:30)*. Thus it is that Jews who reject Christ remain in bondage to Satan and, unless they repent, will go to eternal hell and damnation.

Jesus Prophesied Desolation for Earthly Jerusalem

Think of it. Paul taught that the Jewish people of earthly Jerusalem are in bondage and are "cast out" of God's Kingdom. *Revelation 11:8* says that earthly Jerusalem is spiritual "Sodom and Egypt." Jesus absolutely confirms these scriptures by His own prophecy regarding Jerusalem and her people, the physical Jews. You can read it in *Matthew 23:37-39*, where Jesus prophesied that because of its bloody murders, its vile wickedness, its crimes against the prophets, and its rejection of the Son of God, earthly Jerusalem and Israel would remain *"desolate"* until He, Christ, returns again.

In bondage, cast out, desolate—this is what the Holy Bible says is the prophetic destiny of earthly Jerusalem and its people. Only a remnant—the few who repent and have faith in Jesus—will be saved.

But, the Zionists and Judaizers refuse to accept the judgements of God. Instead, they are determined to set up a Judaic Empire on earth and are laboring to build a Great City of Jerusalem for Jewish dominion right now, today, *before* Jesus returns.

Almost daring God to try to stop them, the Zionists and

Judaizers go so far as to teach the pernicious doctrine that all who assist the Jews to build their earthly empire shall be blessed by God. Would God really bless you or me for helping establish and prosper a nation and city that He himself judges to be *"Sodom and Egypt?"* Will He reward heretical Christians who give aid and comfort to those who hate Him and refuse to serve His Son, Jesus Christ?

Witchcraft: Christian Zionists the Devil's Chief Helpers

Christian Zionists, unwittingly in most cases, have become witchcraft evangelists for this satanic and accursed doctrine *(Galatians1)* and are literally working hard to help build an earthly Judaic Empire that will exalt the coming Antichrist *(2 Thes. 2*), making it possible for him to blaspheme God and His heritage. Christian Zionists are the devil's chief helpers!

God Rejects an Earthly Temple, Throne, and Kingdom

Talmudic Jewish rabbis must be gleefully laughing at the stupidity of Zionist Christians. "Oh, how easily deceived they are," the rabbis must be saying of the Judaizers, and "how spiritually inept." "Why," the rabbis snort, "the dumb Zionist Christians are so happy to help us rebuild our Jewish Temple in Jerusalem and set up a Jewish Kingdom, they don't even respect or believe in what their own New Testament teaches. For the martyr Stephen eloquently preached:

> *"Howbeit, the most High dwelleth not in temples made with hands; as saith the prophet.*
>
> *HEAVEN IS MY THRONE, AND EARTH IS MY FOOTSTOOL: WHAT HOUSE WILL YOU BUILD ME? SAITH THE LORD: OR WHAT IS THE PLACE OF MY REST?" (Acts 7:48-49)*

Get that? Heaven alone is God's throne. Indeed, earth—including the earthly city of Jerusalem—is but His footstool!

Tragic it is, but today's politically correct Zionist Christians are in a real bind. They have so exalted and deified the Jewish race and the temporal nation of Israel in the Middle East that, to be consistent, they are forced to attempt to rebuke Christ Himself! It was Jesus who bluntly told the Jews, "Ye are of your father the devil, and the lusts of your father ye will do. He was a murderer from the beginning and abode not in the truth...for he is a liar and the father of it" *(John 8:43-45).*

Zionist Christians today angrily accuse anyone who dares say even one negative word about the Jews of being "anti-semitic haters." So what would they say about Jesus, who described the Jews as "of their father the devil?"

In a strange and monstrous contradiction, today's Zionist Christian Judaizers reverse what Jesus said. Now, the Jews as an entire race are said to be holy. This, even though the Jews continue to reject Christ and even call Him a "bastard" in the Talmud, their book of Jewish law. So, according to the Christian Judaizers, *it is Jesus who lied about the Jews, not the other way around!* Christian Judaizers truly must secretly despise the words of Jesus regarding the Jews and their destiny.

Christians Possess the Promise

What we discover in scripture, then, is that citizenship in God's heavenly Israel and the promise and heritage of Abraham belong to Christians and to no one else. Abraham's seed is not defined by place of physical birth, by race, by national origin, or by physical parentage. The Chosen People of God are made One in Jesus Christ by means of a spiritual miracle, or change, which creates in them an entirely "new creature" *(John 3:3; Galatians 3:16, 26-29).* Flesh or race availeth a man nothing of value for the saved person is spiritually made a "new creature" in God. He is spiritually neither a Jew nor a Gentile, but is the Chosen of God *(1 Peter 1:23; 2:9)*.

The conclusion of the whole matter is this, that Jewish and Gentile supremacists alike are contributing to confusion and chaos in these last days. Their foolish doctrines are wicked, dangerous, fanciful, racially bigoted and unscriptural. The "Israel of God" is the spiritual nation that has God's blessing. This marvelous blessing is not based on DNA or the flesh. Instead, the Israel of God is God's "holy nation;" its people (Christians) are His spiritually born again heritage. All who are Christ's, chosen out of many nations, are made One. As such, they are citizens of the true Zion, residents of that lovely city, heavenly Jerusalem; jointly, they comprise the "Israel of God"—a holy nation.

In sum, God is no respecter of persons. "Whosoever believeth" may come to new birth in Jesus our Saviour and shall inherit Abraham's promise *(Galatians 3:26-29)*. GOD IS NOT A RACIST!

SIXTEEN

Many Christian Zionists and Judaizers are Convinced that the Gospel of Israel is Greater than Jesus and that Jews Need Not Be Evangelized.

Greater Than Jesus

"But I fear, lest by any means, as the serpent beguiled Eve through his subtilty, so your minds should be corrupted from the simplicity that is in Jesus. For if he that cometh preacheth another Jesus, whom we have not preached, or if ye receive another spirit, which ye have not received, or another gospel, which ye have not accepted, ye might well bear with him."
—Apostle Paul
(2 Corinthians 11:3-4)

On a recent *youtube* video that went viral, five or six young Christians, some eighteen to twenty years of age, attending a national evangelical youth conference were asked, "How many of you

165

love Israel?" All of their hands shot straight up. "How many of you would fight and die for the nation of Israel?," they were asked. Again, every hand quickly went up. "And if Israel got into a war with the United States, how many would choose to go and fight *with* Israel against your home country, the United States?" Once again, all (except one) raised their hand, though not with quite so much enthusiasm. One of the youth slowly raised his hand, then brought it down, raised it again, then down. He appeared somewhat taken aback and unable to make a firm decision. Finally, after looking around and seeing all the others' hands raised, he, too, reluctantly—and slowly—raised his as well.

There you have, captured in the one, brief evangelical video, an image of the entire Christian Church today, for indeed, the parents of these young people are, if anything even more pro-Zionist, pro-Israel, pro-Jewish.

The pro-Zionist propaganda being fed to these youth has convinced them that Israel can do no wrong and if it does, it does not matter. They believe they will be blessed to stand by the Jews, even if it means treason against their own country.

President Clinton Pledges to Fight With Israeli Defense Forces

This is the same philosophy expressed by former President Clinton in a speech to the heads of Jewish organizations a few years ago. "If Israel is ever threatened by its enemies, I pledge I will join on the front lines with the Israeli defense forces and fight for Israel."

What makes this fascinating and startling is that as a young man, Bill Clinton fled the U.S.A. for Great Britain to evade military service in the U.S. Armed Forces. A cowardly draft dodger as far as the United States is concerned, the man who went on to become President of the same nation he once so cavalierly ditched, he now pledges undying devotion to the foreign nation of Israel, proclaims his willingness to die for *that* country.

Rahm Emanuel, former White House Chief of Staff and now Mayor of Chicago, one of our largest cities, refused to serve in a U.S.A. uniform during either of the two Persian Gulf Wars. Instead, as a "dual citizen," he chose to join and serve in the Israeli Defense Forces.

Today's evangelical churches and congregations—whether they are Southern Baptist, Pentecostal, or go by any other denominational or non-denominational name—are solidly in Israel's camp. And so are our nation's politicians and government leader. Whatever Israel asks is okay with the evangelical masses. Israel can do no wrong. Moreover, Jews, as an ethnic group and race, are, these Christians believe, "God's Chosen People," forever and without possible revocation. Wherever the Jew lives, in Israel or in the United States, or, say, in Romania, Bulgaria, Argentina, or Japan—he or she is "Chosen" by God, unique, special, to be favored and blessed in all things and in all ways.

Israel, too, as a nation is made up of God's Chosen People, is the "Apple of God's Eye," and is blessed and favored. It is a good, good thing to be Jewish or to be from Israel, that is the overwhelming viewpoint of millions of evangelicals. And these folks aren't lukewarm in their support for Israel, for Jews, and for all things Jewish—they're wild-eyed about it.

Israel Greater Than America and Greater Than Jesus?

The average Christian evangelical has been bombarded all his life by pro-Zionist religious and political propaganda. Still, it is a shock to hear young people so mesmerized by Israeli dogma they literally would, by their own admission, betray and turn against their own country if the choice arose. To them,

Israel's armed forces, funded by the United States, have committed heinous crimes against Palestinians and others.

the Jewish apartheid State of Israel is greater that the constitutional American republic! But as we shall discover, things are worse—much worse than even this. To a growing number of evangelical Christians, *Israel is greater than Jesus!*

Consider those young people on *youtube*. Why, they say they'd fight and die for Israel, and that's without even knowing what the fight is all about. Indeed, being Israel Firsters, if it came to a bloody, fighting war between Israel and America, they'd desert the country that gave them birth and so faithfully and sweetly tended them all these years, bathing them in luxuries and showering them with prosperity and promise. Oh, yes, they'd turn on the red, white, and blue flag and its people in an instant, take up the flag with Satan's six-pointed star and enthusiastically begin wasting (i.e. *killing*) Americans. They'd kill Americans for Israel and think they are serving God, which actually would be a fulfillment of prophecy. As Jesus foretold: *"They will kill you and think they do God service" (John 16:2).*

A lot of Americans—the majority—have no idea of the depth of the evangelicals' iron-strong and unflinching commitment to Israel and to World Jewry. Several years ago I was invited to speak in Springfield, Missouri, at a prophecy conference organized by the Assembly of God's most well known prophecy teacher, Dr. David Allen Lewis. Lewis is a dyed-in-the-wool Zionist, who claims that Jesus is today in heaven a Jewish man in a Jewish body. That's right, Jesus is a fresh and blood Jew up in heaven. Lewis wears one of those Jewish rabbinical beards. In addition to me and a few other Christian speakers, Lewis also invited to the conference the "religious affairs officer" from the Israel Embassy in Washington, DC, and an Israel military general.

My talk turned out to be very controversial because in it, I emphasized that the nation of Israel is not wise to rely on its own armed forces or even the American government for its salvation. "Israel's only hope," I stressed, "is the saving power of Jesus, the Messiah of Israel and the whole world."

Upon delivering these lines, which I thought would be inspirational—and certainly are true—I noticed the rather cool response I got from the audience, and especially the two Israel VIPs—the embassy official and the Israeli general. Glum, blank looks covered the faces of these two Israelis. They quietly left the auditorium and avoided shaking my hand. That evening during a prearranged dinner at a nice local restaurant, Dr. Lewis, the pro-Zionist Assembly of God evangelist and sponsor of the conference, sat with me and Wanda, along with a local pastor and his wife. Lewis somewhat pensively asked me a question. "What," he queried, "do *you* think is the number one problem in the Christian Church today?"

Reflecting a moment, I suggested that the failure of Christian men and women to frequently and with regularity read and study their Bible was possibly the greatest problem in the Church, because, as it says in God's Word, "My people perish for lack of knowledge."

"No," host Dr. Lewis angrily responded. "The number one problem in the Church today is anti-Semitism."

"Anti-Semitism?," I asked. "I'm amazed," I told him, "because most evangelical churches and congregations are very pro-Israel. Zionism is strongly embraced by Christians everywhere. Could you give me an example of what you believe to be anti-Semitism in a church today?"

Dr. Lewis said he could; then suggested to me that Christians who opposed and even demonstrated against the Hollywood movie, *The Last Temptation of Christ*, were "anti-Semites."

Now, I personally opposed that horrible movie, because it

blasphemed Jesus my Lord, portraying him as a fake Saviour, as a man who had sex and lived with Mary Magdalene. This movie, based on a plot by a Freemason and Satanist, the Greek writer Nicholas Kazantsakis, sickeningly twisted the scriptures, defaming Jesus the Messiah. And indeed, many Christians opposed it, including leaders like Pastor Jerry Falwell, televangelist Pat Robertson, *Focus on the Family's* Dr. James Dobson and many others. Rightly so!

It was Dr. Lewis' contention, however, that all who opposed the movie did so simply because they hated the Jew who was head of Universal Studios, a Mr. Wasserman. Now this was a ridiculous notion on Lewis' part. For one thing, I doubt if many Christians even knew who the Chairman of Universal Studios was. Certainly, not one in a thousand had ever heard the name "Wasserman" in all their lives.

But Lewis insisted: Anti-Semitism is prevalent throughout the Christian Church and this objection to *The Last Temptation of Christ* movie proved it beyond a shadow of a doubt!

Given my penchant, I suppose, for being a troublemaker, an honest one at that, and being aghast at Lewis' unseemly and unfair assertion that men and women who opposed the defamation of my Lord and Saviour are anti-Semites and Jew haters, I quietly but firmly interjected: "David, you are the one who appears to be a racist. Are you not a Jewish supremacist, one who exalts and puts Jews above all other races and people?"

"Yes, I suppose I am," he responded, matter-of-factly. A smug and satisfied look blossomed on his face. The man was proud to admit, "Yes, I am a racist, a Jewish supremacist."

I Am Called an Anti-Semite

The remainder of the evening was pleasant enough. But no sooner had I returned to Austin, Texas, my home base, that I got a phone call from a friend. "Are you aware," he asked, "that Dr. David Allen Lewis is on the radio tonight, calling you an anti-Semite? He says you embarrassed two Israeli VIPs that were in attendance at his conference with your comments."

Fascinated, I got out the notes I used for my message in Springfield and reviewed them. Then it hit me: Indeed, in the minds of the radical Zionist Christians and their Israeli guests, I had done a "no, no." I had actually mentioned the name of "Jesus," even been so audacious as to say that "Jesus is the best and only hope of Israel."

Being new to Christian ministry—coming to this field of work after first almost a quarter of a century in the U.S. Air Force and then several years as a high tech consultant and writer—I was not fully cognizant that today's Christian evangelical leaders never, but never, mention the name of Jesus at a mixed-religious affair. And certainly not when Jews are present. They say that is "offensive." I broke their unwritten law. I said the forbidden word *(shh, not too loud)*—"Jesus!" I was in their eyes an anti-Semite for having done so.

And I figured, my opposition to the blasphemous production, *The Last Temptation of Christ*, further marked me as a Jew-hater and anti-Semite. Stupid, stupid Texe!

Since that auspicious occasion when I discovered I was an anti-Semite, I have continued to offend Jews by mentioning that unmentionable (or so *they* say) name, and I have demonstrated my "stupidity" again and again. Yes, I am—horrors!—a "recidivist anti-Semite."

Warned Not to Preach Against Israel

Since then, I have repeatedly experienced the (to me) exceedingly strange and mysterious, pro-Zionist conduct of Christian leaders regarding their unerring respect and admiration of Israel, the Jews and Judaism, the religion of the

Jews. I have been warned over and over by evangelical pastors, ministry leaders, and layman not to ever say one negative word about Israel, the Jews, or Judaism, for fear that God would curse me, as punishment. Because I go on my way and do so in spite of the warnings and admonishments every day, my mail bears witness that I am under this supposed curse.

"Your Destiny Rests on Your Stand on Israel"

One Church of God leader, Pastor Joseph Chambers of Paw Creek Ministries in North Carolina, wrote in his publication, *End Times and Victorious Living*, that I was surely going to hell for not praising and enthusiastically favoring Israel and its people over all others. He insisted that when a person dies, he or she goes before the throne of God—this is the White Throne Judgement—and is asked *only one question:* "What did you do about my people, Israel?"

In *Christian Zionism—Roadmap to Armegeddon*, an exceptionally well-reasoned and documented volume exposing the fallacies and dangers of Christian Zionism (which I do not think is actually "Christian"), Stephen Sizer, Vicar of Christ Church in Surrey, England and Chairman of the International Bible Society (UK), demonstrates that Dr. Chambers' unorthodox Zionist attitude—and his misreading of scripture— is not at all uncommon among the growing legions of Judaizer "shock troops" willing to "fight and die" for Israel, but not for America. He notes the teachings of Derek Prince, popular among Zionist Christians, whose book, *Last Word on the Middle East*, warns that, "When God comes to judge the nations, he will judge them on their response to the re-gathering of Israel."

This takes it to the next level. Chambers, Prince, and their ilk say that a person's eternal destiny evolves around the issue of whether or not he or she embraces Zionism and zealously supports Israel. Prince and his associates claim that entire nations are in jeopardy and any who oppose the "re-gathering of Israel," that is the return of Jews to Palestinian lands and the conquest and ethnic cleansing of the same, is headed for hell and damnation—they will be "judged" and found guilty by almighty God.

M.R. DeHaan heartily agrees. In his classic judaizer book *Daniel the Prophet*, DeHaan insisted:

> "The solution of this world's ills lies in one formula: bring God's Covenant people (world Jewry) into God's Holy Land...there can be no peace in this world until the nation (the people) and the land are again united...The key to lasting peace is the land of Israel and the Israel of the land..."

Now this is strange, since almost every other Christian Zionist leader says that "Jacob's Trouble," an unparalleled time of war, bloodshed, and tribulation, will ensue once Israel "returns." But since most of the Ashkenazi Jews (Khazars) who immigrated to Israel never had lived there before, how can they return? Moreover, it is commonly taught that at Armageddon, two-thirds of all the returned Jews will be slaughtered. The future of "returned" Jews is bleak if these prophecy teachers are correct.

In any case, DeHaan, like the others, is convinced that anyone who opposes the Jews "returning" to the land of Israel (*nee* Palestine), or even does not assist them to return, is going to have to answer to God. David Brickner, of the Jews for Jesus organization, warns that those who have aligned themselves against Israel "will be judged and delivered into the abyss" (*Future Hope*, p. 108).

Our Blessed Hope: Jesus or Israel?

Stephen Sizer comments:

> "The implication is clear: while the historic
> churches believe that the judgment will be based
> on how people have responded to the claims of
> Jesus, dispensationalists (i.e. Christian Zionists
> and Judaizers) appear to make *Israel* the decisive
> factor. How people and nations have responded to
> Israel's territorial claims and whether they have
> assisted or resisted Jewish emigration to Palestine
> will determine, in whole or in part, their eternal
> destiny.

> This deduction logically follows from the premise
> (by the Christian/Zionists) that Israel enjoys a
> separate and superior covenant, purpose, and
> destiny on earth. To the church; they remain
> God's Chosen People." (*Christian Zionism—Road
> to Armegeddon*, p. 201)

Sizer is on target. The Christian Zionists believe the Old
Covenant that God "exclusively made with Israel" is far
superior and overrules the New Covenant Jesus made with the
whole world. Of course, in Paul's letter to the Hebrews, he
flatly calls the New Covenant a "better" covenant and shows
that the Old Covenant made with Israel was not only flawed,
but "decayeth and is vanishing." But when did the Zionist
zealots ever start reading the scriptures? Moreover, they also
smugly hold the books of the Old Testament to be superior to
those of the New Testament—If this is not so, then why do
they so rudely and inappropriately dismiss virtually everything
Paul wrote in his letters to the Hebrews, Romans, Galatians,

Colossians?

Paul's emphasis continually is on Jesus and the cross, while that of the Zionists is on Israel and the Jewish race. Sizer is therefore reluctantly forced to conclude that for the Zionist heretics—that's what they are, heretics—"Jesus is devalued, salvation and judgement redefined, and Israel sacralized" (that is, made into a religious idol).

Sizer further concludes: "Indeed, it could be argued that if Israel is actually the measure for, and mediator of, ultimate peace, then 'blessing' Israel has, for some Christian Zionists at least, become synonymous with or even more important than simply believing in Jesus. It is the new Gospel."

Remember the old "Got milk" advertisements? Well, with the Zionists, it's "Got Israel?," because if you do, you're fixed for eternity. You're on your way to heaven. There, you'll live in harmony and love with all the Jews who have ever lived, because Jews don't go to hell. Their Talmud says that's not possible for Jews because the whole of their race is divine.

Every Jew Who Ever Lived Goes to Heaven

Arno Froese, founder of Midnight Call and Friends of Israel Ministries, once actually told me, without a trace of jocularity about his statement, that on Judgement Day, every Jew who ever lived would be resurrected from the dead and would automatically, *en masse*, be redeemed. Their previous status, he said, is immaterial: murderer, rapist, adulterer, sodomite, molester of little children, even hater of Jesus, it does not matter.

According to Froese, this good deal only applies to the Jews. They get a free pass solely because of their bloodline. Gentiles have to pay the piper and will be judged for each and every sin. Most will suffer eternal damnation, but not Jews. They are favored and blessed, so all go to heaven.

Froese's fanatical pro-Zionist teachings make me shake my head, considering their blatantly pompous racist premise. One wonders how many Jews Froese has sent to hell by telling them they do not need to convert, they'll all get Jesus in the next life automatically after they're miraculously reborn and redeemed.

I suspect that South Carolina's Arno Froese has no idea that Jewish rabbis, in their Talmud, teach their synagogue congregations that there is no heaven, and that this planet earth shall someday become a Jewish Utopia and Paradise. Yes, both their Talmud and Kabbalah hold out for World Jewry a future, perfect world right here on earth in which the Jews shall rule and reign, be rich and enjoy every manner of fleshly pursuit, and, incidentally, put most Gentiles to death, for good measure.

Hebrew A Heavenly Language?

Froese is more extreme in his Zionist philosophy than are many other Christian Zionists. He doesn't trust English language Bibles. Only Bibles written in Hebrew are perfect, he claims, because Hebrew is a heavenly and perfect language. The Bible cannot be translated accurately by men into other flawed languages. John Hagee has also bought into this idea that Hebrew is the heavenly language. Hagee insists that even God and the angels speak Hebrew in heaven. This is a crazy notion since the world's top linguist scientists have proved that all human languages are derivatives and combinations of other existing, as well as extinct, languages, and there is no such thing as a "pure" language, at least here on earth.

But what makes Arno Froese's and John Hagee's belief and teaching about the Hebrew language scriptures being the only trustworthy and accurate version is that the entire New Testament was written and came to us in the *Greek* language.

The Jews and Israel, of course, hated and made war on the writers of the Gospels and other books of the New Testament and by no means were willing to publish it in Hebrew. Indeed, in our era, some Orthodox Jewish rabbis encourage devout Jews to *burn* all copies of the New Testament that come into their possession, and there are published news accounts of entire Jewish communities in towns and villages coming together to have book-burning bonfires of New Testaments.

The inescapable conclusion is that Froese disrespects and demeans Bible truth as given to the world by God in His New Testament. A great part of His Word are the admonitions of Jesus and the Apostles to go forth into all the world—into *all* nations, including Israel—and preach the Gospel, the cross of Jesus, and the Kingdom of God. Christ Jesus, the Bible teaches, is foundation, cornerstone, head and King.

Christianity Has Nothing of Value for Jews

This is the Great Commission, which Arno Froese and other Zionists discount and which is the reason why Froese contends—as he privately stated to me at a Prophecy Conference in Niagara Falls, New York—"Christianity has *nothing* of value to offer the Jews. We must not and should not preach to the Jews."

Christianity has "nothing of value" to offer the Jews? Jesus is what we offer—true Christians, including me, are not ashamed of Jesus and the Gospel, for as it says in *Romans*, it is the "power unto salvation."

This Zionist message espoused by Froese and the extreme Zionist supporters of Israel is from the pit of hell. It is a Gospel of doom and death for Jews. It is a monstrous philosophy that, in the guise of being philosemitic (pro-Jewish) is, in fact, a dogma designed to foster *hatred* of Jews. It is an anti-Semitic philosophy to its core, one which excludes Jews from the marvelous opportunity for eternal salvation, even from the joy of having Christ in their hearts. What misery such a dogma brings the Jews. Satan loves Christian Zionism.

Incidentally, I asked Arno Froese what he thought about Jewish Christian groups, such as *Jews for Jesus*, whose mission is heavily centered on the evangelizing of Jews *by* saved Jews. "A horrible group," he responded.

Finally, just out of interest, I asked Froese about the passages in *Revelation 2* and *3* warning of the anti-Christian crimes and ungodly acts of the "Synagogue of Satan."

"Oh, don't bring those scriptural passages up," he advised. "Don't get into that. No one really knows what that means. It probably applies to false Christian groups, not to Jews."

A very predictable answer by a Zionist/Judaizer who refuses to believe that Jews can be of Satan, regardless of Jesus' statement to the contrary in *Matthew ("Ye are of your father the devil...")*. Indeed, as I have shown, it is Froese's contention that the New Testament is itself impossibly flawed and not to be trusted as it was not written down in Hebrew by its authors, but in Greek, the common language at the time.

So, as far as the Great Commission, for Froese and his many counterparts we should simply adopt the dumbed-down simpleton approach by exclaiming, "Great Commission?... What Great Commission?"

Why preach to the Jews, as once did Jesus, Peter, James, and other holy men of God? The Jews' salvation is assured, guaranteed, pre-ordained. They're home free. Don't waste your time on reaching them for Jesus. Walk on by.

In today's religion of Christian Zionism, the mythical land of Holy Israel so dominates the landscape that millions of evangelicals can no longer understand why Jesus prophesied in *Matthew 23* the fall and destruction of Jerusalem and Israel—an event which occurred exactly as he had forecast, in 70 AD.

Nor can many evangelicals figure out why Peter and others were once brought before the Sanhedrin and ordered by the chief rabbis to stop their preaching of Jesus. (Peter responded: "We must obey God and not man" and went right on preaching Jesus to the Jews).

For that matter, why did the first Christian martyr, Stephen, preach Jesus to the Jews? After all, it made them so angry and stirred them up so much they attacked and murdered him! Why did he give his life for what many Christian Zionist evangelicals today consider a worthless cause—preaching Jesus to his fellow Jews?

Indeed, if Lewis, Hagee, Froese, and countless other Judaizers are right and the Gospel of Israel is greater than the Gospel of Jesus, then Christ our Lord Himself was an utter fool to willingly die on the cross. What for?—to save Jews who do not need saving!

Is Fleshly, Physical Israel Greater Than the Church?

Stephen Sizer laments in his excellent book, *Christian Zionism—Road-map to Armageddon*, of the tenets of the Zionists and Judaizers, "Israel is elevated to a status above the church...Israel will replace the church on earth...whole nations will be blessed through association with, and support of Israel..."

Sizer emphasizes that, "This view is entirely at variance with the New Testament...which makes choseness conditional on faith in Jesus."

In the fast-growing "New" Gospel of Christian Zionism, he reports, "promises by Jesus and the New Testament writers are generally ignored, and the State of Israel is sacralized (put on a pedestal, elevated, and revered as a supreme religious idol), the consummation of God's purposes on earth rather than the astonishing work of Christ and his redeemed church... The sacralizing of Zionism ultimately subordinates the cross... and the evangelical focus by Christian Zionism is placed upon a restored Jewish kingdom rather than the body of Christ, and upon the contemporary State of Israel rather than the cross of Christ."

Another Spirit and Another Gospel

What we have, then, is what the Apostle Paul warned is "another spirit" and "another gospel" (see *2 Corinthians 11:3-4*) which masquerade as holy truth but, in fact, horribly degrade and demean Jesus Christ and elevate the things of this earth (carnal Israel and the fleshly tribe, or race, of Jews) to a superior status of idolatry and mythical superstition.

It is significant that Paul cautioned the church that if a person comes preaching this new gospel, he should be soundly rejected and the simplicity of the Gospel of Jesus always be remembered and embraced.

Sizer also points out that the Zionist dogma of the Jews about not needing or being covered by the New Testament but remaining under the restrictions and confines of the Old Covenant and the law is so alien to the true and traditional Christian as to be both absurd and apostasy. Paul, the writer of Hebrews, warned that a return to the shadows of the Old Covenant is apostasy, for to their loss, they are crucifying the Son of God all over again and subjecting him to public disgrace. Sizer therefore repudiates nationalistic Zionism and sadly regrets the fact that this apostasy has unfortunately become dominant and even pervasive among evangelical churches, ministries, and denominations.

Zionists Lift-Up Israel, Not Jesus

We have a raging apostasy and heresy within our very midst.

A fundamental change has taken place in a brief few decades which has severely damaged and which continues to wreak havoc on the Christian faith and its redemptive message. Jesus said, "If I be lifted up, I will draw all men to me." The Zionists lift up not Jesus but world Jewry and Israel. Their message of Israel *alpha* and *omega* has taken many churches by storm and has turned tens of millions away from the profound, life-giving message of Jesus and the cross.

For the Christian Zionist, the Gospel of Israel is greater than the Gospel of Jesus..

SEVENTEEN

Christianity Has No Jewish Roots

"I am Alpha and Omega, the first and *the* last"
—Revelation 1:11

Most churches and Christian ministries today have a "Doctrinal Statement," a declaration in which the founders or the members list and perhaps, explain and elaborate on their essential beliefs. The large denominations—Southern Baptist, Methodist, Lutheran, Presbyterian, Seventh Day Adventists, etc.—have entire volumes and books dedicated to explaining the group's beliefs and dogma. But even smaller organizations have at least a paper or booklet, or maybe a one-page summary of the organization's basic beliefs.

It is interesting to note that a growing number of evangelical Christian churches and ministers state and emphasize their so-called *"Jewish roots."* Some flatly state that their group's goal is to "return to Christianity's Jewish roots."

Return? Frankly, having repeatedly scoured the scriptures,

184 O TEXE MARRS

I cannot find that Christianity ever *had* "Jewish roots."
Certainly today, Christianity is as far from Judaism as black is
from white and male is from female. Of course, there are those
of a sinister and perverted nature who enthusiastically seek to
mix black and white and whose goal is to integrate the male
and female ends of the spectrum.

Our reigning Masonic culture and the *Zeitgeist* (Spirit) of
our time, based as they are on universalism and relativism,
make this terrible mistake and by so doing, are unleashing
diabolical psychopathologies and nihilism into society.

In truth, Judaism and Christianity sit at different ends of
the reality spectrum and for this reason, a term like Judeo-
Christianity is both an oxymoron and, when actually
implemented, produces an abominable combination.

Jesus Came From Heaven

We are often told that Jesus was a Jew and that, therefore,
Christianity is of Jewish origins. Now, while Jesus came in the
flesh first to the Jews, and the bearer (Mary) of the Christ child
was of the tribe of Judah, Jesus Himself was not and is not a
"Jew." Jesus is, in fact, a man out of time. He has no age, no
birth, no earthly country of citizenship, and though He is a
King, His subjects ultimately owe fealty and loyalty to no
distinguishable terrestrial nation or kingdom.

While the Gospels give the genealogy of Jesus' blood
lineage, in fact they do so only so that we, mere human beings,
can situate Jesus' coming and His native parentage within the
context of human patterns. In fact, Jesus did not come from
His earthly "father," Joseph's, sperm, or from His mother,
Mary's, egg. There was no human conception. Instead the
Holy Spirit, say the scriptures "overshadowed" Mary and the
"seed" was implanted in her by God: "for that which is
conceived in her is of the Holy Ghost" *(Matthew 1:20).*

We read further:

*"Now the birth of Jesus Christ was on this wise:
when as his mother was espoused to Joseph, before
they came together, she was found with child of the
Holy Ghost."*

Joseph, Mary's husband was told of Mary's role in the
birth of Christ by an angel sent by God, who appeared to him
in a dream and told him that Mary was with child not by man
but by the Holy Ghost; That is, the Spirit of God:

*"And she shall bring forth a son, and thou shalt call
his name JESUS: for he shall save his people from
their sins.*

*Now all this was done, that it might be fulfilled
which was spoken of the Lord by the prophet,
saying,*

*Behold, a virgin shall be with child, and shall bring
forth a son, and they shall call his name Emmanuel,
which being interpreted is, God with us.*

*Then Joseph being raised from sleep did as the
angel of the Lord had bidden him, and took unto
him his wife:*

*And knew her not till she had brought forth her
firstborn son: and he called his name JESUS."*
(Matthew 1:21-25)

In the Gospel of John, we are told that Jesus was not

created first on earth but was with God in the beginning:

"In the beginning was the Word, and the Word was with God, and the Word was God.

The same was in the beginning with God." (John 1:1 and 2)

Not only that, but the Bible reveals that Jesus, the Word, who was in the beginning with God, was the one who *created* all things. Yes, you understood me right. Jesus, who is one with God and is God, created the universe, including our galaxy, our planet and its life forms. As we read in *1 John 5:7:*

"For there are three that bear record in heaven, the Father, the Word, and the Holy Ghost: and these three are one."

So, the Holy Ghost (also called the Holy Spirit) is one with Jesus, the Son of God, and God the Father. It was He who overshadowed the Virgin Mary and made it possible for the miracle of Jesus coming in the flesh as God:

"And the Word was made flesh, and dwelt among us, (and we beheld his glory, the glory as of the only begotten of the Father), full of grace and truth." (John 1:14)

Jesus Not a Jew in Heaven

When you and I hear a man or woman who claims to be Christian speak a lie and say that Jesus was a Jew, we should politely and kindly, yet with firmness, correct him or her. I have even had Christian pastors and evangelists assert to me that Jesus is in heaven today, bodily as a Jew. This is sacrilege. This is the desacrilizing of the Son of God. It is blasphemy to teach that the Son of God is a Jew, or for that matter, of any human DNA.

When a person does this, what he is doing is attempting to strip god and His Son of their majesty and glory, and I for one am angered at such diabolism, even when the offending party is sincere.

It is not right to attempt to bring God down to our mortal level. Consider the witness of the Apostle John, as found in *Revelation 1:9-18:*

"I John, who also am your brother, and companion in tribulation, and in the kingdom and patience of Jesus Christ, was in the isle that is called Patmos, for the word of God, and for the testimony of Jesus Christ.

I was in the Spirit on the Lord's day, and heard behind me a great voice, as of a trumpet,

Saying, I am Alpha and Omega, the first and the last: and, What thou seest, write in a book, and send it unto the seven churches which are in Asia; unto Ephesus, and unto Smyrna, and unto Pergamos, and unto Thyatira, and unto Sardis, and unto Philadelphia, and unto Laodicea.

And I turned to see the voice that spake with me. And being turned, I saw seven golden candlesticks;

And in the midst of the seven candlesticks one like

*unto the Son of man, clothed with a garment down
to the foot, and girt about the paps with a golden
girdle.*

*His head and his hairs were white like wool, as
white as snow; and his eyes were as a flame of fire;*

*And his feet like unto fine brass, as if they burned in
a furnace; and his voice as the sound of many
waters.*

*And he had in his right hand seven stars: and out of
his mouth went a sharp twoedged sword: and his
countenance was as the sun shineth in his strength.*

*And when I saw him, I fell at his feet as dead. And
he laid his right hand upon me, saying unto me,
Fear not; I am the first and the last:*

*I am he that liveth, and was dead; and, behold, I am
alive for evermore, Amen; and have the keys of hell
and of death.*

Does this describe a mere man to you, whether Jew or
Gentile? John had, years earlier, walked the dusty streets of
cities and towns with Jesus, in his coming in the flesh to fulfill
His mission. The disciple John had laid his head on Jesus'
breast. Who knew or would recognize the resurrected Jesus
better than John? Yet, at Patmos, beholding the magnificent
visage before him, so overwhelmed and overcome was John
that he writes:

"And when I saw him, I fell at his feet as dead."

Jesus Came From "Land of the Gentiles"

Now many of the Jews disrespected Jesus and refused to consider him as their prophesied Messiah because Jesus had not been born in Jerusalem. He came from the lowly city of Nazareth and was a Galilean. The scriptures note that Galilee was known by the Jews as the "land of the Gentiles." Could the Messiah have come from the land of the Gentiles? No! Not according to the dogmatic rabbis.

The scriptures also say that Joseph was instructed by the angel of the Lord to name the Christ child Jesus, "for he shall save his people from their sins."

Meditate on that: Jesus shall save his people "from their sins." Who are *"His people?"* Jesus was and is omniscient. He knows all things before they happen. It is true that He first preached to the Jews who were said to be "His own," but were *they* "his people?"

Once, while preaching to a crowd, his disciples noticed that his mother and brothers had come and wanted to speak with him. They told Jesus, and here was the Lord's amazing response:

> *"But he answered and said unto him that told him, Who is my mother? and who are my brethren?*
>
> *And he stretched forth his hand toward his disciples, and said, Behold my mother and my brethren!*
>
> *For whosoever shall do the will of my Father which is in heaven, the same is my brother, and sister, and mother." (Matthew 12:48-50)*

Here we have, therefore, a divine principle which Jesus Himself set forth; "Whosoever that doeth the will of God is

Jesus' brother, sister, and mother. If we believe in Jesus Christ and are of Him, then we are his children, his family; we may address Him as "Abba, Father."

We Are Sons and Daughters

All who spiritually are of Jesus also become the sons and daughters of God and we are fellow citizens of that Holy City, Heavenly Jerusalem, the City of God. We and we alone are the Elect, God's Chosen. Peter said that the mercy of God and the resurrection of His Son, Jesus Christ, from the dead, is such that we who have faith are the blessed recipients:

"Blessed be the God and Father of our Lord Jesus Christ, which according to his abundant mercy hath begotten us again unto a lively hope by the resurrection of Jesus Christ from the dead,

To an inheritance incorruptible, and undefiled, and that fadeth not away, reserved in heaven for you,..." *(1 Peter 1:3-4)*

"But ye are a chosen generation, a royal priesthood, an holy nation, a peculiar people; that ye should shew forth the praises of him who hath called you out of darkness into his marvellous light:

Which in time past were not a people, but are now the people of God: which had not obtained mercy, but now have obtained mercy." *(1 Peter 2: 9-10)*

The word "generation" in the King James Version of the Holy Bible means *offspring, ethnic group, race, nation, or people.* Yes, Christians are the Chosen People of God, His nation.

Now being "God's Chosen" has nothing to do with "Jewish roots." It truly sickens me to come into contact with "Christians" who smugly think they are superior to other Christians because, they boast, "they have been on a pilgrimage to the Nation of Israel."

Some people measure their spirituality by how often they visit Jerusalem or whether or not they observe the Jewish Holy Days and festivals.

So-called Messianic Christians are particularly prone to such foolish boasting, and many attend what they describe as "Christian Synagogues" where they dance and observe Jewish customs and rituals. They even call their ministers "rabbi," in spite of the fact that Jesus instructed us not to do this, for the word "rabbi" means master and is reserved for God alone.

One wonders if these Judaizer types believe that in acting Jewish, they will be blessed more than are other Christians.

Born Again Are "Heirs to the Promise"

The Apostle Paul correctly taught us that all who are God's Chosen People are heirs according to the promise given Abraham. Indeed, we are the very seed of Abraham and this is so because we are *born again (John 3:3)* in Christ Jesus. Our bloodline, our specific physical or earthly race, or our Jewishness in practice, is of no importance whatever—whether Jew or Greek (Gentile), all are one through faith.

"For ye are all the children of God by faith in Christ Jesus.

For as many of you as have been baptized into Christ have put on Christ.

There is neither Jew nor Greek, there is neither

bond nor free, there is neither male nor female: for
ye are all one in Christ Jesus.

And if ye be Christ's, then are ye Abraham's seed,
and heirs according to the promise." (Galatians
3:26-29)

Accursed and Bewitched Judaic Gospel

Where, then are the "Jewish roots" of Christianity? Paul, in
writing to the Church at Galatia, in Greece, taught that all
things were like "dung" (fertilizer) to him except the cross of
Jesus. Any other Gospel than that—He was speaking of the
Judaic law and religion—was an *"accursed"* gospel *(Galatians*
1:8-9), and those who practiced an accursed gospel were
"bewitched" (Galatians 3:1).

Paul knew of the Jews' heresy, that some were attempting
to bring the saved Gentiles back into the bondage of Judaism
by mixing their "Jewish roots" with the received Gospel of the
cross of Jesus. Paul bluntly declared this was "accursed" and
"bewitched."

In *Hebrews,* Paul wonderfully explains that the Old
Covenant, given to Moses and the prophets, "decayeth and
waxeth old:"

"For if that first covenant had been faultless, then
should no place have been sought for the second.

For finding fault with them, he saith, Behold, the
days come, saith the Lord, when I will make a new
covenant with the house of Israel and with the house
of Judah:

Not according to the covenant that I made with their

*fathers in the day when I took them by the hand to
lead them out of the land of Egypt; because they
continued not in my covenant, and I regarded them
not, saith the Lord.*

*For this is the covenant that I will make with the
house of Israel after those days, saith the Lord; I
will put my laws into their mind, and write them in
their hearts: and I will be to them a God, and they
shall be to me a people:*

*And they shall not teach every man his neighbour,
and every man his brother, saying, Know the Lord:
for all shall know me, from the least to the
greatest...*

*In that he saith, A new covenant, he hath made the
first old. Now that which decayeth and waxeth old is
ready to vanish away. (Hebrews 8:7-13)*

With Jesus' coming, humanity was presented with a "better
covenant." Jesus became the centerpoint, the focus of all
praise and worship. No more would the sacrificial blood of
bulls and of goats suffice:

*"Neither by the blood of goats and calves, but by
his own blood he entered in once into the holy
place, having obtained eternal redemption for us.*

*For if the blood of bulls and of goats, and the ashes
of an heifer sprinkling the unclean, sanctifieth to the
purifying of the flesh:*

How much more shall the blood of Christ, who

through the eternal Spirit offered himself without spot to God, purge your conscience from dead works to serve the living God?

And for this cause he is the mediator of the new testament, that by means of death, for the redemption of the transgressions that were under the first testament, they which are called might receive the promise of eternal inheritance...

So Christ was once offered to bear the sins of many; and unto them that look for him shall he appear the

The Judaic religion has been called "the most horrible religion on Earth."

second time without sin unto salvation." (Hebrews 9:12-15, 28)

The New Covenant is written on men's hearts and the Jewish festivals and holy days and the veneration of the earthly city of Jerusalem are neither mandatory nor even necessary components of this New Covenant (see *Romans 14*), for Christ has *perfected* those who He had sanctified:

"For by one offering he hath perfected for ever them that are sanctified. Whereof the Holy Ghost also is a witness to us: for after that he had said before, This is the covenant that I will make with them after those days, saith the Lord, I will put my laws into their hearts, and in their minds will I write them; And their sins and iniquities will I remember no more." (Hebrews 10:14-17)

"But now they desire a better country, that is, an heavenly: wherefore God is not ashamed to be called their God: for he hath prepared for them a city." (Hebrews 11:16)

King of the Jews?

Returning to Jesus, the author and finisher of our faith, we may ask the question, did Jesus come in the flesh intending to be coronated as *"King of the Jews?"* The answer is clear: No, he did not!

When asked by Pontius Pilate, the Roman Governor, "are you a king?" Jesus answered, that yes, he is a king, but *"My kingdom is not of this world."*

Once, in the wilderness for forty days, Satan came to Jesus and gave him a vision of all the great kingdoms of earth. The

Adversary told Jesus that if he would bow down and worship him, Satan, all this would be his. To which Jesus responded: *"Thou shalt not tempt the Lord thy God."*

Yes, Jesus is King, and his subjects are the angels, all the host of heaven, and every human being that He has adopted through faith as his son or daughter. Jesus' kingdom is real and incomparable to any earthly kingdom. And the Jews were offered *that* kingdom—not the puny earthly kingdom for which they lusted, but the magnificent Kingdom of God Almighty. They refused. Instead, they went so far in their wickedness as to crucify the very Son of God.

Now read of Jesus' judgement of the Jews as regards the kingdom of God:

> *"Jesus saith unto them, Did ye never read in the scriptures, The stone which the builders rejected, the same is become the head of the corner: this is the Lord's doing, and it is marvellous in our eyes?*
>
> *Therefore say I unto you, The kingdom of God shall be taken from you, and given to a nation bringing forth the fruits thereof.*
>
> *And whosoever shall fall on this stone shall be broken: but on whomsoever it shall fall, it will grind him to powder.*
>
> *And when the chief priests and Pharisees had heard his parables, they perceived that he spake of them.*
>
> *But when they sought to lay hands on him, they feared the multitude, because they took him for a prophet." Matthew 21:42-46*

Kingdom Taken From the Jews

Oh, how bitter this pill is for the Jews and their Christian Judaizer friends in evangelical churches to swallow. The kingdom is taken from the Jews, and the House of Israel is *"left desolate"* (see *Matthew 23:39*). It is given to another Nation "bringing forth the fruits thereof."

That righteous nation, as we have learned, is made up of all—Jew *or* Gentile—who are Christ's. Yes, even a "remnant" of the Jews shall be saved; if they believe in the Gospel and have faith in Jesus, they will be "graffed" back in: "And so all Israel (Jew, Gentile) shall be saved."

This refers, however, to the "Israel of God;" that is Paul's description in *Galatians 6*. It is true that the scriptures say that "Salvation is of the Jews" but this simply means that it was through this nation that God saw fit to usher in the Kingdom of God through faith in His Son, Jesus.

The Jews, as inhabitants of earth—like you and I are also—cannot save; their Judaism religion in fact, is from the pits of hell, and Jesus thus told the Pharisees, *"Ye are of your father the devil" (John 8:44)*.

We thank God, however, for the prophets and disciples who were of Israel and who demonstrated their faith to us as an example. In this way, salvation is of the Jews. But keep in mind that the Jewish nation, the House of Israel, were the ones who *killed and persecuted* the prophets and the saints, so be careful and be modest in your praise. They are but men and women who, like all of us, need Jesus for salvation.

How to Clear Up Confusion

I recognize that many Christians are confused about this matter. They are confused because of the propaganda and lies taught by their pseudo-Christian pastors and theologians. It is far better, dear friends, for you and I to study the Word of God for ourselves. Let the Holy Spirit be our preacher and instructor and we cannot err.

Do not be suckered-in by the Judaizers. The Orthodox Rabbis are using these deceived teachers to sow confusion and error in the Christian Church.

Jesus, not the ancient or modern earthly nation of Israel, must be our focus. Do not elevate the Jews to high status. Elevate God and His Son, Jesus, to first place in your life. Jesus is "the Way, the Truth, and the Life." He is the "Light of the World," and our Saviour and Lord.

I leave you with two amazing Scriptures on which to meditate. When someone comes and attempts to lead you astray by emphasizing your so-called "Jewish roots," it is well to remind them of these two passages.

First, that Jesus is eternal, was with God from the beginning and has declared to all: *"I am Alpha and Omega, the first and the last..." (Revelation 1:11)*. Second, that Jesus Christ came in the flesh as "Immanuel, God with us" over two thousand years ago, being born to a virgin in the little city of Bethlehem. He is, *"the Lamb slain from the foundations of the world." (Revelation 13:8)*

That, dear friends, is mind-boggling is it not? Possibly the human brain is not engineered to fathom such a fact, but the man or woman filled with the Holy Ghost certainly can understand this glorious truth. Jesus had no Jewish roots. He came from Heaven, for He is Alpha and Omega, the first and the last; He is the Lamb slain from the foundation of the world.

EIGHTEEN

Confusion Abounds When You Enter the Realm of Judaism, the Jews, and Israel

Clear Up All the Confusion

A woman named Sara recently wrote me quite an epistle. After accusing me of being a Jew hater, an anti-Semite and a few other choice names, Sara explained to me what I needed to do to rectify my situation. I must, she said, "get in touch with my Hebraic roots." Moreover, Sara insisted that my ministry should emphasize the "Jewishness of Christianity." Also that I should become active in promoting Israeli political causes.

To be honest, in due respect to Sara, I don't believe I have any "Hebraic roots" I can get in touch with. Being sort of a "Heinz 57" type of racial genotype, the only ancestral roots I can trace go back to Scotland. But I really don't care to return to any Scottish roots, so I'll stick to my American roots, thank you.

As far as emphasizing the "Jewishness" of Christians, that seems a little odd to me. Jesus gave his Great Commission to us to go into all the world and preach the Gospel. It says in *Galatians 3:29* that regardless of race or national origin, etc., "If ye be Christ's, then are ye Abraham's seed and heirs according to the promise." So, I am Abraham's seed by virtue of belonging to Christ through faith. The wonderful thing about the Christian faith is it is for *everyone*: Whosoever will may come.

Of course, I love the books of the Old Testament because their prophecies point to the power of God and the glory of Jesus. And there's really very little in them about "Jews" or "Jewishness." Here at *Power of Prophecy* our emphasis is on "Jesusness," not "Jewishness." He is our central focus, our end goal, our guide.

Sara further suggested several ways I could emphasize "my Jewish roots." One, I should regularly encourage people to "pray for the peace of Jerusalem." I could also have the blowing of a shofar to open my radio program, have a Jewish singer deliver a song in Hebrew, and encourage trips by Christians to the Holy Land.

Especially, said Sara, I must never, never again criticize the modern nation of Israel or its people, the Jews. Doing that, Sara emphatically suggested, puts "a pall of death on my ministry" because God will curse me for not continually blessing the Jews.

Sara's letter is not exceptional; I've seen worse. Take Ted's, for example. Ted also says I am an anti-Semite. He also brands me a "liar" because I have stated that the Jewish Talmud is ungodly and is man-made tradition. Not so, said Ted, indeed, Jesus often read from the Talmud in the synagogue and so did his apostles.

I suspected he had the Talmud confused with the Old

Testament which Jesus did read from in the Synagogue. The teaching of the Talmud, which is today the Jews' most holy book, held more reliable and better than the Old Testament, is diametrically opposite to the principles set forth in the Old Testament. And whereas the books of the Old Testament are written by holy men of God by inspiration and are thus God's Word, the books of the Talmud were written by Jewish rabbis, and some of them were remarkably evil and sinister, not to mention devilish in lifestyle.

I really wanted to write Ted and let him know that there was no printed Talmud back in Jesus' day, but I figured it would just rile him more.

Most who write to me contend that the "Jews are God's Chosen People" and eternally will be, no matter what they do or say, and no matter what crimes a Jew might commit. Take Kelly, for instance, who wrote to me and touted the Jews. As *Kelly* put it, Jews are already forgiven before they even commit a sin, unlike what happens to us, mere Gentiles. They never have to ask for forgiveness, Kelly added, their covenant covers them from the cradle to death.

Wow! Now that is a good deal, isn't it? Forgiven forever from the moment of birth.

I emailed Kelly back and asked whether, if she and I converted to Judaism, we could get this same great coverage.

Kelly's response was interesting. She said she'd never thought about that before, but as converts to Judaism, probably we would not be covered by the Eternal Covenant because, she figured, "It is a blood thing. You have to be born to Jewish parents."

A natural response by me might have been to ask whether just one birth parent who was a Jew would do, and if so, must it be the father or the mother, but I decided that would be too cheeky and unfair of me. Besides, it'd be a great waste of my time.

To my surprise, a week later, Kelly mailed me again to inform me that she had spoken by phone to a rabbi in her home city of Seattle, and he told her that if a Gentile converts to Judaism, he or she was a "real Jew." Conversion to Judaism gave them "permanent salvation." Kelly had even discussed this with her pastor, a Bible Church fellow, who told her the rabbi was correct, that by following the Law of Moses, the Gentile convert to Judaism would be saved.

The pastor, according to Kelly, also advised her that in the New Testament, Paul says that, "All Israel shall be saved." That, he stated would mean *all* Israel, including converts to Judaism, no matter their sin or spiritual condition.

Interesting, if this pastor is right (but, he's not), inclusion— that is, conversion—into the *religion* of Judaism automatically gives a man or woman spiritual absolution as well as citizenship in the nation of Israel.

Well, the Orthodox Jewish rabbis who determine for the Israeli government who can be a citizen and who cannot wouldn't agree with that. Moreover, how can a person's religion entitle that person to become a member, or citizen, of a nation? Can an Ethiopian who converts to Christianity thereby claim American citizenship, since America, some say, is a "Christian nation?" Does the fact that so many today describe Israel as a "Jewish State" confer citizenship to Jews everywhere, including converts to the Jewish religion? Entertainer Sammy Davis, Jr. converted to Judaism. So did Marilyn Monroe. Were they the seed of Abraham, his descendants? Were they Israeli citizens? Their biographies say no, they remained American.

Kelly's emails continued. I had to admire her tenacity in attempting to resolve this thorny matter. She said in one that some friends had told her that membership in a Messianic

Synagogue—you know, one of those popular new Christian Zionist worship congregations where the Pastor is called "rabbi" and they engage in Davidic ritual dancing, observe all the Jewish feast days, wear yarmulkes and shawls, etc.— confers on a person eternal salvation. This, they assured her is because, as a member of such a synagogue, the Christian is covered by the eternal covenant, and this covenant is irreversible. God would not welch on his promises.

This possibility of being guaranteed eternal life by membership in a "Christian Synagogue" was important to Kelly because, as a strict Pentecostal, she was persuaded a Christian could lose his/her salvation if they sinned "too much." But perhaps her sins would not count against her if she joined a Messianic Synagogue.

I then asked (tongue in cheek) if possibly a better way to "acquire" eternal salvation might be for her to *renounce* her Christian faith entirely and convert to the old fashioned Jew type of Judaism. That way, she could become both a Jew and a citizen of Israel. She had expressed her "unbounding love for Israel" in her previous emails, so I know she preferred Israel over any other nation, including her native U.S.A.

Kelly said that would be a problem. She loved Jesus, you see, and couldn't give *Him* up. Of course not, I responded, but maybe you can convert to Judaism and bring Jesus with you. Kelly then phoned and asked the rabbi, who said, "Absolutely not. There is no Jesus in Judaism and there never will be!" (The rabbi told the truth).

Back to the Messianic Synagogue option Kelly went. She confided to me that visiting that congregation, she fell in love with the dancing, the Hebrew music, the prayers in Hebrew. All of it. *This*, she said, was authentic Christianity and Judaism combined, and the best part was that, finally, although she is a Gentile (English heritage and blood for centuries in her genealogy), she can now express her "Hebraic roots." This, said Kelly, must be the emotions which the early Christian Church felt. (Not quite Kelly, not the Churches in Greece, say, or in Rome or Turkey).

Kelly's infatuation with "things Jewish" and her desire to observe each and every one of the Jewish high holy days and festivals—Rosh Hashanah, Sukkoth, Passover, and so forth—are shared by many who write to me. Not a few have warned that *unless* I observe these holy days, I cannot be a genuine or strong Christian. Some flat out tell me I'm going to hell if I don't observe them. It's a sin not to do so.

For goodness sake, Lord Jesus, I do wish these folks would actually *read* your Word. That sure would clear up some things for them. Here's what Paul wrote, in *Colossians 2*:

So-called "Messianic Christian" congregations bring ignorant people back under the Law.

"And this I say, lest any should beguile you with enticing words... As ye have therefore received Christ Jesus the Lord, so walk ye in him... Beware lest any man spoil you through philosophy and vain deceit, after the tradition of men...and not after Christ... And ye are complete in him... Let no man therefore judge you in meat, or in drink, or in respect of an holyday, or of the new moon, or of the Sabbath days. Which are a shadow of things to come, but the body is of Christ."

Does that clear things up for anyone?

Not a day goes by that I am not also reminded of *Genesis 12:3* which, the writer or caller invariably claims, states that whoever blesses *the Jews*, God will bless. Strange because I have read that same verse over and over, and actually, it never changes. The Jews are not mentioned there at all! What it *really* says is that whoever blesses *Abraham* will be blessed and whoever curses Abraham will be cursed.

Galatians 3:29 says that Abraham's seed is all who belong to Jesus, Jew and Gentile! Besides, Abraham was a Babylonian, from Ur in the Chaldees, not a Jew.

These terrible Hobson's Choices about Judaism, Jews, Israel, and so forth seem to bedevil many Christians today. Pat Robertson, founder of *The 700 Club*, stated in a talk show that Jews could enter Heaven if they perfectly followed the Law. (Not true: Paul taught us that a person cannot be saved and enter heaven by obeying the law, that only through faith in Jesus is this attained).

Famous evangelist and crusader Billy Graham stated on TV (Robert Schuller's *Hour of Power*) that sincere Jews already have Jesus in their hearts whether they know it or not and whether or not they have ever read the Holy Bible.

Evidently this was his private interpretation of scripture, but exactly what passage of scripture teaches this? I can't find any.

Graham's contention made me wonder why it is he bothers to preach at all. I phoned his ministry's headquarters in Minneapolis to ask that very question, and they kindly advised me that Billy Graham does not "single out any specific religion and seek converts from that religion." But, what about reaching Jews in general, I asked, Jews that decided to go, say, to a Billy Graham Crusade and then decided to walk the aisle to make a "decision for Christ," as Billy puts it?

Well, said the nice Billy Graham Ministry assistant, in that case, "we send the person back to his or her hometown rabbi." And if the person doesn't have a rabbi, I queried? Then, said the Graham aide, "we provide names and addresses of local synagogues, and rabbis for that person to go to."

Somewhat apoplectic and holding back a scream and howl of displeasure, I managed to get out the words, "Uh, won't that synagogue or that rabbi just tell the person that he or she does *not* need Jesus and that, anyway, Jesus, according to the Jews' Talmud, is a "blasphemer," a "fornicator," a "liar" now burning in Hell and a traitor to the Jews?

"That is a possibility," the Billy Graham official agreed. "Still, we've done our part. That's all we can do as Christians. What else can we do?"

Good question. As *Christians*, what should Billy Graham and his Ministry do when a Jew says, "I want to make a decision for Christ." Should that person be immediately referred to a synagogue and rabbi who does *not* believe in Christ and who probably *despises* Christ?

Seven Things to Know

Well, dear reader, I would like to comment on all these rather confusing situations and shed light and profundity on them. The best way to do this is by going to the scriptures, for in them we find unshakable, unchanging truth. Indeed, the keys to the Gospel itself are discovered in the scriptures.

Before we begin, may I ask if whether you sense, as do I, that there is massive confusion in Christendom today on these topics? Bring up the subject of the Jews, their religion, and the nation of Israel, and things seem to go berserk. People's opinions and beliefs are all over the map. The Devil, not God, is the author of confusion, so let's just clear up all the devilish confusion.

First, salvation is by grace, not by obeying the Jewish laws. "Knowing that a man is not justified by the works of the law, but by the faith of Jesus Christ, even we have believed in Jesus Christ...for by the works of the laws shall no flesh be justified" *(Galatians 2:16)*.

Second, in God's plan of salvation, there is no distinction of race, ethnicity, or blood: "There is neither Jew nor Greek… for ye are all one in Christ Jesus. And if ye be Christ's, then are ye Abraham's seed, and heirs according to the promise" *(Galatians 3:28-29)*.

Third, focus on Jesus Christ and him alone; worship Him every day 24/7. The Sabbath was to be a day of man resting in God—a day of rest. Jesus is our rest; in him we find peace. It is not a matter of which day. Centering on a particular day diverts a man from the *One* whom the day is intended to honor—Our Lord Jesus: "One man esteemeth one day above another: another esteemeth every day alike. Let every man be fully persuaded in his own mind. He that regardeth the day regardeth it to the Lord" *(Romans 14:5-6)*.

Also, please, remember that Jesus said that He is Lord of the Sabbath. It's not the other way around: "And ye are complete in him which is the head of all principality and power...blotting out the handwriting of ordinances that was against us, which was contrary to us, and took it out of the way, nailing to his cross...Let no man, therefore, judge you ... in respect of a holy day...or of the Sabbath days" *(Colossians 2:10-16)*.

Fourth, God couldn't care less about your support or nonsupport of Israel or any country or for any earthly citizenship or attainment to any given nation: Paul said, "For God forbid that I should glory, save in the cross of our Lord Jesus, by whom the world is crucified unto me."

Thus, you don't get credit—or demerits—from god for embracing and exalting Jerusalem, Israel or the United States. The prophets and holy men of God confessed that they were "strangers and pilgrims on the earth, but they desired a better country, that is, an heavenly...ye are come unto Mount Sion, and unto the City of the Living God, the heavenly Jerusalem for here (on earth) we have no continuing city, but we seek one to come" *(Hebrews 11, 12, and 13)*.

Fifth, faith in Jesus Christ, which is magnanimously offered to all, is sufficient and that faith has nothing to do with whether one adopts the Jewish culture (or American, or Mexican, or...) or returns to "Hebraic roots," or holds on to something carnal called "Jewishness," and so we are to embrace Jesus and his salvation and obey the Holy Spirit which God therefore places in our heart: "Love not the world, neither the things that are in the world. If any man love the world, the love of the Father is not in him. For all that is in the world, the lust of the flesh, and the lust of the eyes, and the pride of life, is not of the Father, but is of the world. And the world passeth away, and the lust thereof: but he that doeth the will of God abideth forever" *(1 John 2: 15-17)*.

Sixth, the Old Covenant once offered the Jews was broken by them and no longer exists. If they had kept it, it would still be in existence today but it is not (*Hebrews 8* and *9*). Jesus is the bearer of a "new and better covenant."

"...He is the mediator of a better covenant, which was established upon better promises. For if that first covenant had been faultless, then no place should have been sought for the second. For finding fault with them, he said, Behold, the days come, saith the Lord, when I will make a new covenant with the House of Israel and with the House of Judah. Not according to the covenant that I made with their fathers...Because they continued not in that covenant" *(Hebrews 8:5-9)*.

"In that he saith, a new covenant he hath made the first old. Now that which decayeth and waxeth old is ready to vanish away...Which stood only in meats and drinks, and diverse washings, and carnal ordinances, imposed on them until the time of reformation *(Jesus' coming!)*. But Christ being come an high priest of good things to come, by a greater and better tabernacle...for this cause he is the mediator of the new covenant, that...they which are called might receive the promise of eternal inheritance" *(Hebrews 8:13; 9:10-15)*.

Seventh and final, it is not possible for a believer in Judaism who rejects Jesus as Lord and Saviour to be saved or enter heaven.

Faith in Jesus and that alone is necessary for heaven, and if a Jew (or Gentile) does not have Jesus, the Son of God, he doesn't have God the Father, either: "And this is the record, that God hath given to us eternal life, and this life is in his Son. He that hath the Son hath life; *and* he that hath not the Son of God hath not life."

"And we know that the Son of God is come, and hath given us an understanding, that we may know him that is true, and we are in him that is true, even in his Son Jesus Christ. This is the true God, and eternal life." *(1 John 5:11-12 and 20)*

Is The Confusion Ended?

I truly hope that all who were confused about the subject of the Jews, Judaism, Israel, "Jewishness," "Hebraic roots," the Jewish holy days, and eternal salvation, are now of clear and undivided mind. But I have to admit: I'm not holding my breath. Seems as if most folks just don't really care what God's word really says.

Please remember always what Paul said—never forget the "simplicity of the Gospel," Christ, and Him crucified for our sins. Don't be brought into bondage by what the scriptures call the "weak and beggarly elements" *Galatians 4:9-11*, which are but style and culture rather than substance.

Some, I suppose, prefer to call me derisive names like "Jew hater: or "anti-Semite." That's okay, I can take the heat. It's all worth it if I have helped even one confused soul to come away with a clear mind. And, I might add: If you remain confused and bewildered about these weighty things we have discussed, my advice is that you forget everything you have been told by me and everybody else. Yes, toss most all of it away in the Sea of forgetfulness and remember just the *one* word that *really* counts: *Jesus*.

Is that clear?

The Jews, Khazaria, and the Kol Nidre Oath

By Benjamin Freedman

These comments were made by Benjamin Freedman in a letter to Dr. David Goldstein, LLD, of Boston, dated Oct. 10, 1954. They are printed here in part. The entire letter is published in the book, *Facts Are Facts*. Benjamin Freedman, a Jew and former owner of the Woodbury Soap Company, spent much of his considerable fortune to expose the encroaching Jewish tyranny.

You will probably also be astonished as the 150,000,000 Christians years ago when I electrified the nation with the first publication by me of the facts disclosed by my many years of research into the origin and the history of the so-called or self-styled "Jews" in eastern Europe. My many years of

Benjamin Freedman

intensive research established beyond the question of any doubt, contrary to the generally accepted belief held by Christians, that the so-called or self-styled "Jews" in eastern Europe at any time in their history in eastern Europe were never the legendary "lost ten tribes" of Bible lore. That historic fact is incontrovertible.

Relentless research established as equally true that the so-called or self-styled "Jews" in eastern Europe at no time in their history could be correctly regarded as the direct lineal descendants of the legendary "lost ten tribes" of Bible lore. The so-called or self-styled "Jews" in eastern Europe and modern history cannot legitimately point to a single ancestor who ever even set a foot on the soil of Palestine in the era of Bible history. Research also revealed that the so-called or self-styled "Jews" in eastern Europe were never "Semites," are not "Semites" now, nor can they ever be regarded as "Semites" at any future time by any stretch of the imagination. Exhaustive research also irrevocably rejects as a fantastic fabrication the generally accepted belief by Christians that the so-called or self-styled "Jews" in eastern Europe are the legendary "Chosen People" so very vocally publicized by the Christian clergy from their pulpits.

Maybe you can explain to me, my dear Dr. Goldstein, the reason why and just how the origin and the history of the Khazars and Khazar Kingdom was so well concealed from the world for so many centuries? What secret mysterious power has been able for countless generations to keep the origin and the history of the Khazars and Khazar Kingdom out of history text-books and out of classroom courses in history throughout the world? The origin and history of the Khazars and Khazar kingdom are certainly incontestable historic facts and also establish beyond any question of doubt the origin and history of the so-called or self-styled "Jews" in eastern Europe.

The origin and history of the Khazars and Khazar kingdom and their relationship to the origin and early history of the so-called or self-styled "Jews" in eastern Europe was one of history's best kept secrets until wide publicity was given in recent years to my research on this subject. Do you not think, my dear Dr. Goldstein, that it is time this whole subject was dragged out of its hiding place?

In the year of 1948 in the Pentagon in Washington I addressed a large assembly of the highest officers of the United States Army in the G2 branch of military intelligence on the highly explosive geopolitical situation in eastern Europe and the Middle East. Then as now, that area of the world was a potential threat to the peace of the world and to the security of this nation. I explained to them fully the origin of the Khazars and Khazar Kingdom. I felt then as I feel now that without a clear and comprehensive knowledge of that subject it is not possible to understand or to evaluate properly what has been taking place since 1917, the year of the Bolshevik Revolution in Russia. It is the "key" to that problem.

Upon the conclusion of my talk a very alert Lieutenant Colonel present at the meeting informed me that he was the head of the history department of one of the largest and highest scholastic rated institutions of higher education in the United States. He had taught history there for 16 years. He had recently been called back to Washington for further military service. To my astonishment he informed me that he had never in all his career as a history teacher or otherwise heard the word "khazar" before he heard me mention it there. That must give you some idea, my dear Dr. Goldstein, of how successful that mysterious secret power was with their plot to "black out" the origin and the history of the Khazars and Khazar Kingdom in order to conceal from the world and particularly Christians the true origin and the history of the so-called or self-styled "Jews" in eastern Europe.

The Russian conquest in the tenth through thirteenth centuries of the little-known-to-history Khazars apparently ended the existence for all time of the little-known-to-history 800,000 square mile sovereign kingdom of the so-called or self-styled "Jews" in eastern Europe, known then as the Khazar Kingdom. Historians and theologians now agree that this political development was the reason for the *"Important Change in the Wording of the 'Kol Nidre'"* by Meir ben Samuel in the eleventh century, and for the policy adopted by the so-called or self-styled "Jews" that *"The Law of Revocation in Advance was Not Made Public."* Will you be patient with me while I review here as briefly as I can the history of that political emergence and disappearance of a nation from the pages of history?

Prior to the tenth century the Khazar Kingdom had already been reduced by Russian conquests to an area of about 800,000 square miles. As you will observe on this map reproduced from the Jewish Encyclopedia the territory of the Khazar in the tenth century was by far the largest of any in Europe. The population of the Kingdom was made up for the most part of the Khazars with the addition of the remnants of the populations of the 25 peaceful agricultural nations that had inhabited this approximate 1,000,000 square miles before their conquest by the invading Khazars. In the first century B.C. the Khazars invaded eastern Europe from their homeland in Asia. The

Khazars invaded eastern Europe via the land route between the north end of the Caspian Sea and the south end of the Ural Mountains.

The Khazars were not "Semites." They were an Asiatic Mongoloid nation. They are classified by modern anthropologists as Turco-Finns racially. From time immemorial the homeland of the Khazars was in the heart of Asia. They were a very warlike nation. The Khazars were driven out of Asia finally by the nations in Asia with whom they were continually at war. The Khazars invaded eastern Europe to escape further defeats in Asia. The very warlike Khazars did not find it difficult to subdue and conquer the 25 peaceful agricultural nations occupying approximately 1,000,000 square miles in eastern Europe. In a comparatively short period the Khazars established the largest and most powerful kingdom in Europe, and probably the wealthiest also.

The Khazars were a pagan nation when they invaded eastern Europe. Their religious worship was a mixture of phallic worship and other forms of idolatrous worship practiced in Asia by pagan nations. This form of worship continued until the seventh century. The vile forms of sexual excesses indulged in by the Khazars as their form of religious worship produced a degree of moral degeneracy the Khazar's king could not endure. In the seventh century King Bulan, ruler at that time of the Khazar Kingdom, decided to abolish the practice of phallic worship and other forms of idolatrous worship and make one of the three monotheistic religions, about which he knew very little, the new state religion. After a history session with representatives of the three monotheistic religions, King Bulan decided against Christianity and Islam and selected as the future state religion the religious worship then known as "Talmudism,: and now known and practiced as "Judaism." This event is well documented in history.

King Bulan and his 4,000 feudal nobles were promptly converted by rabbis imported from Babylonia for that event. Phallic worship and other forms of idolatry were thereafter forbidden. The Khazar kings invited large numbers of rabbis to come and open synagogues and schools to instruct the population in the new form of religious worship. It was now the state religion. The converted Khazars were the first population of so-called or self-styled "Jews" in eastern Europe. So-called or self-styled "Jews" in eastern Europe after the conversion of the Khazars are the descendants of the Khazars converted to "Talmudism," or as it is now known "Judaism," by the mass conversion of the Khazar population.

After the conversion of King Bulan, none but a so-called or self-styled "Jew" could occupy the Khazar throne. The Khazar Kingdom became a virtual theocracy. The religious leaders were the civil administrators also. The religious leaders imposed the teachings of the Talmud upon the population as their guide to living. The ideologies of the Talmud became the axis of political, cultural, economic and social attitudes and activities throughout the Khazar kingdom. The Talmud provided civil and religious law.

It might be very interesting for you, my dear Dr. Goldstein, if you have the patience, to allow me to quote for you here from Volume IV, pages 1 to 5, of the Jewish Encyclopedia. The Jewish Encyclopedia refers to the Khazars as "Chazars." The two spellings are optional according to the best authorities. The two are pronounced alike. Either Khazar or "Chazar" is pronounced like the first syllable of "costume" with the word "Czar" added onto it. It is correctly pronounced "*cos*(tume) Czar." The Jewish Encyclopedia has five pages on the Khazars but I will skip through them:

"CHAZARS: A people of Turkish origin whose

life and history are interwoven with THE VERY BEGINNINGS OF THE HISTORY OF JEWS OF RUSSIA... driven on by the nomadic tribes of the steppes and by THEIR OWN DESIRE FOR PLUNDER AND REVENGE... In the second half of the sixth century the Chazars moved westward... The kingdom of the Chazars was firmly established in MOST OF SOUTH RUSSIA BEFORE THE FOUNDATION OF THE RUSSIAN MONARCHY BY THE VARANGIANS (885)... At this time the kingdom of the Chazars stood at the height of its power AND WAS CONSTANTLY AT WAR... At the end of the eighth century... the chagan (king) of the Chazars and his grandees, TOGETHER WITH A LARGE NUMBER OF HIS PEOPLE; EMBRACED THE JEWISH RELIGION... The Jewish population in the entire domain of the Chazars, in the period between the seventh and tenth centuries, MUST HAVE BEEN CONSIDERABLE... about THE NINTH CENTURY, IT APPEARS AS IF ALL THE CHAZARS WERE JEWS AND THAT THEY HAD BEEN CONVERTED TO JUDAISM ONLY A SHORT TIME BEFORE... It was one of the successors of Bulan named Obadiah, who regenerated the kingdom and STRENGTHENED THE JEWISH RELIGION. He invited Jewish scholars to settle in his dominions and founded SYNAGOGUES AND SCHOOLS. The people were instructed in the Bible, Mishnah, and the TALMUD and in the 'divine service of the hazzanim'... In their writings the CHAZARS

USED THE HEBREW LETTERS... THE
CHAZAR LANGUAGES PERDOMINATED...
Obadiah was succeeded by his son Isaac; Isaac by
his son Moses (or Manasseh II); the latter by his
son Nisi; and Nisi by his son Aarron II. King
Joseph himself was a son of Aarron, AND
ASCENDED THE THRONE IN ACCORDANCE
WITH THE LAW OF THE CHAZARS
RELATING TO SUCCESSION... The king had
twenty-five wives all of royal blood, and sixty
concubines, all famous beauties. Each one slept in
a separate tent and was watched by a eunuch...
THIS SEEMS TO HAVE BEEN THE
BEGINNING OF THE DOWNFALL OF THE
CHAZAR KINGDOM... The Russian Varangians
established themselves at Kiev...until the final
conquest of the Chazars by the Russians... After
a hard fight the Russians conquered the
Chazars... Four years later the Russians
conquered all of the Chazarian territory east of
the Azov... Many members of the Chazarian
royal family emigrated to Spain... Some went to
Hungary, BUT THE GREAT MASS OF THE
PEOPLE REMAINED IN THEIR NATIVE
COUNTRY."

The greatest historian on the origin and the history of the
so-called or self-styled "Jews" in eastern Europe was Professor
H. Graetz, himself a so-called or self-styled "Jew." Professor
H. Graetz points out in his famous "History of the Jews" that
as so-called or self-styled "Jews" in the Khazar Kingdom, they
believed these converted Khazars to be the "lost ten tribes."
These rumors were no doubt responsible for the legend which

grew up that Palestine was the "homeland" of the converted Khazars. On page 141 in his "History of the Jews" Professor H. Graetz states:

> "The Chazars professed a coarse religion, which was combined with sensuality and lewdness... After Obadia came a long series of Jewish Chagans (kings) for ACCORDING TO A FUNDAMENTAL LAW OF THE STATE, ONLY JEWISH RULERS WERE PERMITTED TO ASCENT THE THRONE... For some time THE JEWS OF OTHER COUNTRIES HAD NO KNOWLEDGE OF THE CONVERSION OF THIS POWERFUL KINGDOM TO JUDAISM, and when at last a vague rumor to this effect reached them, THEY WERE OF THE OPINION THAT CHAZARIA WAS PEOPLED **BY THE REMNANT OF THE FORMER TEN TRIBES.**"

When Khazars in the first century B.C. invaded eastern Europe their mother-tongue was an Asiatic language, referred to in the Jewish Encyclopedia as the "Khazar languages." They were primitive Asiatic dialects without any alphabet or any written form. When King Bulan was converted in the seventh century, he decreed that the Hebrew characters he saw in the Talmud and other Hebrew documents were thereupon to become the alphabet for the Khazar language. The Hebrew characters were adopted to the phonetics of the spoken Khazar language. The Khazars adopted the characters of the so-called Hebrew language in order to provide a means for providing a written record of their speech. The adoption of the Hebrew characters had no racial, political or religious implication.

The western European uncivilized nations which had no alphabet for their spoken language adopted the alphabet of the Latin language under comparable circumstances. With the invasion of western Europe by the Romans, the civilization and the culture of the Romans was introduced into these uncivilized areas. Thus the Latin alphabet was adopted for the language of the French, Spanish, ENGLISH, Swedish and many other western European languages. These languages were completely foreign to each other yet they all use the same alphabet. The Romans brought their alphabet with their culture to these uncivilized nations exactly like the rabbis brought the Hebrew alphabet from Babylonia to the Khazars when they introduced them in the form of the Talmud's alphabet.

Since the conquest of the Khazars by the Russians and the disappearance of the Khazar Kingdom the language of the Khazars is known as Yiddish. For about six centuries the so-called or self-styled "Jews" of eastern Europe have referred to themselves while still resident in their native eastern European countries as "Yiddish" by nationality. They identified themselves as "Yiddish" also. There are today in New York City as you know, my dear Dr. Goldstein, many "Yiddish" newspapers, "Yiddish" theatres, and many other cultural organizations of so-called or self-styled "Jews" from eastern Europe which are identified publicly by the word "Yiddish" in their title.

Before it became known as the "Yiddish" language, the mother-tongue of the Khazars added many words to its limited ancient vocabulary as necessity required. These words were acquired from the languages of its neighboring nations with whom they had political, social or economic relations. Languages of all nations add to their vocabularies in the same way. The Khazars adapted words to their requirements from the German, the Slavonic and the Baltic languages. The

Khazars adopted a great number of words from the German language. The Germans had a much more advanced civilization than their Khazar neighbors and the Khazars sent their children to German schools and universities.

The "Yiddish" language is not a German dialect. Many people are led to believe so because "Yiddish" has borrowed so many words from the German language. If "Yiddish" is a German dialect acquired from the Germans, then what language did the Khazars speak for the 1000 years they exited in eastern Europe before they acquired culture from the Germans? The Khazars must have spoken some language when they invaded eastern Europe. What was that language? When did they discard it? How did the entire Khazar population discard one language and adopt another all of a sudden? The idea is too absurd to discuss. "Yiddish" is the modern name for the ancient mother-tongue of the Khazars with added German, Slavonic and Baltic adopted and adapted numerous words.

"Yiddish" must not be confused with "Hebrew" because they both use the same characters as their alphabets. There is not one word of "Yiddish" in ancient "Hebrew" nor is there one word of "Hebrew" in "Yiddish." As I stated before, they are as totally different as Swedish and Spanish which both likewise use the same Latin characters for their alphabets. The "Yiddish" language is the cultural common denominator for all the so-called or self-styled "Jews" in or from eastern Europe. To the so-called or self-styled "Jews" in or from eastern Europe, "Yiddish" serves them like the English language serves the populations of the 48 states of the United States. Their cultural common denominator throughout the 48 states is the English languages, or wherever they may emigrate and resettle. The English language is the tie which binds them to each other. It is the same with the "Yiddish" language and so-called or self-styled "Jews" throughout the world.

"Yiddish serves another very useful purpose for so-called or self-styled "Jews" throughout the world. They possess in "Yiddish" what no other national, racial or religious group can claim. Approximately 98% of the world's so-called or self-styled "Jews" living in 42 different countries of the world today are either emigrants from eastern Europe, or their parents emigrated form eastern Europe. "Yiddish" is a language common to all of them as their first or second language according to where they were born. It is an "international" language to them. Regardless of what country in the world they may settle in they will always find co-religionists who also speak "Yiddish." "Yiddish" enjoys other international advantages too obvious to describe here. "Yiddish" is the modern language of a nation, which has lost its existence as a nation. "Yiddish" never had a religious implication, although using Hebrew characters for its alphabet. It must not be confused with words like "Jewish." But it is very much.

Directly north of the Khazar Kingdom at the height of its power a small Slavic state was organized in 820 A.D. on the south shore of the Gulf of Finland where it flows into the Baltic Sea. This small state was organized by a small group of Varangians from the Scandinavian peninsula on the opposite shore of the Baltic Sea. The native population of this newly formed state consisted of nomad Slavs who had made their home in this area from earliest recorded history. This infant nation was even smaller than our state of Delaware. This newly-born state however was the embryo which developed into the great Russian Empire. In less than 1000 years since 820 A.D. this synthetic nation expanded its borders by ceaseless conquests until it now includes more than 9,500,000 square miles in Europe and Asia, or more than three times the area of continental United States, and they have not stopped.

During the tenth, eleventh, twelfth, and thirteenth centuries the rapidly expanding Russian nation gradually swallowed up the Khazar kingdom, its neighbor directly to the south. The conquest of the Khazar kingdom by the Russians supplies history with the explanation for the presence after the thirteenth century of the large number of so-called or self-styled "Jews" in Russia. The large number of so-called or self-styled "Jews" in eastern Europe after the destruction of the Khazar Kingdom were thereafter no longer known as Khazars but as the "Yiddish" populations of these many countries. They so refer to themselves today.

In the many wars with her neighbors in Europe after the thirteenth century Russia was required to cede to her victors large areas which were originally part of the Khazar Kingdom. In this manner Poland, Lithuania, Galicia, Hungary, Rumania, and Austria were acquired from Russia territory, originally a part of the Khazar Kingdom. Together with this territory the nations acquired a segment of the population of so-called or self-styled "Jews" descended from the Khazars who once occupied the territory. These frequent boundary changes by the nations in eastern Europe explains the presence today of so-called or self-styled "Jews" in all these countries who all trace their ancestry back to the converted Khazars. Their common language, their common culture, their common religion, and their common racial characteristics classify them all beyond any question of doubt with the Khazars who invaded eastern Europe in the first century B.C. and were converted to "Talmudism" in the seventh century.

The so-called or self-styled "Jews" throughout the world today of eastern European origin make up at least 90% of the world's total present population of so-called or self-styled "Jews." The conversion of King Bulan and the Khazar nation in the seventh century accomplished for "Talmudism," or for "Judaism" as "Talmudism" is called today, what the conversion of Constantine and the western European nations accomplished for Christianity. Christianity was a small, comparatively unimportant religious belief practiced principally in the eastern Mediterranean area, until the conversion to the Christian faith of the large populations of the western European pagan nations after the conversion of Constantine. "Talmudism" the civil and religious code of the Pharisees, most likely would have passed out of existence like the many other creeds and cults practiced by the peoples in that area before, during and after "Pharisaism" assumed its prominent position among these creeds and cults in the time of Jesus. "Talmudism," as "Pharisaism" was called later, would have disappeared with all its contemporary creeds and cults but for the conversion of the Khazars to "Talmudism" in the seventh century. At that time "Talmudism" was well on its way towards complete oblivion.

In the year 986 A.D. the ruler of Russia, Vladimir III, became a convert to the Christian faith in order to marry a Catholic Slavonic princess of a neighboring sovereign state. The marriage was otherwise impossible. Vladimir III thereupon also made his newly-acquired faith the state religion of Russia, replacing the pagan worship formerly practiced in Russia since it was founded in 820 A.D. Vladimir III and his successors as the rulers of Russia attempted in vain to convert his so-called or self-styled "Jews," now Russian subjects, to Russia's Christian state religion, and to adopt the customs and culture of the numerically pre-dominant Russian Christian population. The so-called or self-styled "Jews" in Russia refused and resisted this plan vigorously.

They refused to adopt the Russian alphabet in place of the Hebrew characters used in their "Yiddish" language. They resisted the substitution of the Russian language for "Yiddish" as their mother-tongue. They opposed every attempt to bring about the complete assimilation of the former sovereign

Khazar nation into the Russian nation. They resisted with every means at their disposal. The many forms of tension which resulted produced situations described by history as "massacres," "pogroms," "persecution," discrimination etc.

In Russia at that period in history it was the custom as in other Christian countries in Europe at that time to take an oath, vow or pledge of loyalty to the rulers, the nobles, the feudal landholders and others in the name of Jesus Christ. It was after the conquest of the Khazars by the Russians that the wording of the "Kol Nidre" (All Vows) prayer was regarded as the "law." The effect of this *"LAW OF REVOCATION IN ADVANCE"* obtained for all who recited it each year on the eve of the Day of Atonement divine dispensation from all obligations acquired under "oaths, vows and pledges" to be made or taken in the *COMING YEAR.* The recital of the "Kol Nidre" (All Vows) prayer on the eve of the Day of Atonement released those so-called or self-styled "Jews" from any obligation under *"oaths, vows or pledges:* entered into during the *NEXT TWELVE MONTHS.* The *"oaths, vows and pledges"* made or taken by so-called or self-styled "Jews" were made or taken with *"tongue in cheek"* for twelve months.

The altered version of the "Kol Nidre: (All Vows) prayer created serious difficulties for the so-called or self-styled "Jews" when its wording became public property. It apparently did not remain a secret very long, although the Talmud states, *"the law of revocation in advance was not made public."* The altered version of the "Kol Nidre" (All Vows) prayer soon became known as the "Jews Vow" and cast serious doubt upon "oaths vows or pledges" given to Christians by so-called or self-styled "Jews." Christians soon believed that "oaths, vows or pledges" were quite worthless when given by so-called or self-styled "Jews." This was the basis for so-called "discrimination" by governments, nobles, feudal landholders,

226 O TEXE MARRS

and others who required oaths of allegiance and loyalty from those who entered their service.

All intelligent attempt was made to correct this situation by a group of German rabbis in 1844. In that year they called an international conference of rabbis in Brunswick, Germany. They attempted to have the "Kol Nidre" (All Vows) prayer completely eliminated from the Day of Atonement ceremonies, and entirely abolished from any religious service of their faith. They felt that the secular prologue to the Day of Atonement ceremonies was void of any spiritual implication and did not belong in the synagogue ritual. However, the preponderant majority of the rabbis attending that conference in Brunswick came from eastern Europe. They represented the congregations of Yiddish-speaking, so-called or self-styled "Jews" of converted Khazar origin in eastern Europe. They insisted that the altered version of the "Kol Nidre" (All Vow) prayer be retained exactly as it was then recited on the Day of Atonement. They demanded that it be allowed to remain as it had been recited in eastern Europe since the change by Meir ben Samuel six centuries earlier. It is today recited in exactly that form throughout the world by so-called or self-styled "Jews." Will the 150,000,000 Christians in the United States react any differently when they become more aware of its insidious implications?

How genuine can the implications, inferences and innuendoes of the so-called "brotherhood" and "interfaith" movements be under these circumstances? These so-called movements are sweeping the nation like prairie fires. If the Talmud is the axis of the political, economic, cultural and social attitudes and activities of so-called or self-styled "Jews" participating in these two so-called movements, how genuine are the "oaths, vows or pledges" taken or given in connection with these two so-called movements by so-called or self-styled

"Jews?" It would be a superlative gesture of "brotherhood" or of "interfaith" if the National Conference of Christians and Jews succeeded in expunging from the Talmud all anti-Christ, anti-Christian, and anti-Christianity passages. At a cost of many millions of dollars the National Conference of Christians and Jews succeeded in expunging from the New Testament passages which so-called or self-styled "Jews" regarded as offensive to their faith. A great portion of the cost was supplied by so-called or self-styled "Jews." Christians might now supply funds to expunge from the Talmud passages offensive to the Christian faith. Otherwise the so-called "brotherhood" and "interfaith" movements are merely mockeries.

Blood Secrets of the Synagogue of Satan

by Texe Marrs

One group and one group alone is responsible for virtually all wars and bloodshed on the face of this planet. This evil cabal is few in numbers but, like a deadly octopus, its tentacles reach out to grip and strangle untold multitudes of innocent victims. The initiates of every secret society and internationalist organization, from the Council on Foreign Relations and the Jesuits to the Bilderbergers and the Order of Skull & Bones, obey the dictates of this sinister group and tremble when standing before its leaders.

The cabalist group I refer to is the *Synagogue of Satan*, an ancient, yet modern elite so politically powerful and so fabulously wealthy that even past history has been twisted, reshaped, and revised to meet its preferred version of humanity's gloomy, totalitarian future.

Religious and racial in nature, the Synagogue of Satan is,

at its essence, a grotesque, satanic cult. Its high council is composed of High Priests of Lucifer; these are men who literally worship death while practicing sexual magick and occult rituals of the blackest nature.

Regrettably, this Luciferian cabal of high priests is supported by over eighteen million people around the globe who call themselves "Jews." Some of these people, a great many, are fanatical in their support of the Synagogue of Satan. They go by the name, "Zionists." Others provide the Cabal with only token, often nominal, support.

These eighteen million Jews are joined in their often zealous embrace by a great number of Gentiles who are also boastful of being Zionists. While these Gentile supporters are, on the whole, woefully ignorant of the horrific, ultimate goal of the Synagogue of Satan, their support and service to the cause of Lucifer helps drive the global Synagogue of Satan's never-ending successful campaigns of revolution, war, famine, financial calamity, and bloodshed.

Given the proven fact that the elitist High Priests of Lucifer who comprise the Synagogue of Satan and their servants possess ownership of almost every major book publishing firm in the world, rarely is a book or volume ever printed that has the courage and audacity requisite to expose the ongoing conspiracy of this monstrous group.

I am, therefore, extremely pleased to recommend to thinking men and women the excellent volume, *The Synagogue of Satan*, by Britain's Andrew Hitchcock. You will find it to be a useful, revealing, and accurate historical guide to the sinister crimes and dark events that have propelled the Synagogue of Satan to the precipice of world power.

The term *Synagogue of Satan* is biblical in origin. As Mr. Hitchcock notes, the book of Revelation in the Holy Bible minces no words. God warns us of the horrendous and diabolical power to be wielded in the last days by the entity identified as the "Synagogue of Satan."

What is most fascinating, however, is that the scriptures clearly tell us that the evil leaders of this entity are not Jews! Yes, they say they are Jews, and the world recognizes them as Jews, even as "Israel," but they lie! Listen to what God's Word reveals:

> *"I know the blasphemy of them which say they are*
> *Jews, and are not, but are the Synagogue of Satan. "*
> *(Revelation 2:9)*

Mind-boggling, isn't it? These wicked, world power-brokers want us to believe they are Jews; they boastfully lay claim to Israel as their heritage. But, in reality, they are blasphemous liars. What is going on here?

Given the fact that the masters of the Synagogue of Satan today possess such incredible and extraordinary influence over the media, it stands to reason that the average world citizen easily falls for the Lie. People everywhere trust these great and beneficent leaders who say, "We are Jews" to be exactly that: Jews. No wonder the Apostle Paul warned that Satan's disciples come disguised as "ministers of righteousness" and as "angels of light."

In the case of the minions of the Synagogue of Satan, they come to us disguised as "God's Chosen," as "Israel," as the One Race selected by God to produce in the future a Messiah (not Jesus!) for eternity. We are Jews, they proudly boast while, at the same time they suggest that others—that is, the defective lower and inferior races—are obligated by God to bless them, to follow the "Jews" lead, to bow down and serve them as "God's Chosen."

"Yes," they arrogantly explain, "we are Jews, and you are

goyim (cattle), and we have been chosen by divine edict to rule over you and over the entire planet."

Shocking as it is, these claims by the Jewish pretenders of racial superiority, even Super Race consciousness, have for the most part been accepted by Christian evangelicals as legitimate, authoritative, and coming direct from God. Christian evangelicals say it is the lot of the Gentiles to bow down and accord virtual god-like status to the "Jews" and to their newly formed political entity, Israel, lest God be angered and curse and punish those who resist the Jews and their artificially created nation, "Israel."

Sadly, nowhere in the established Christian Church can be found a pastor or evangelist today who has the spiritual wisdom, or even the common sense, to ask the cardinal question, *"Who is this Synagogue of Satan that God warns about in the book of Revelation?"* And nary a soul seems to ask the correlating question, *"Just who are these wicked imposters of whom God warns will say they are "Jews" and are not, but do lie?"*

One thing is for sure—the Bible regards these false, lying Jewish imposters as dangerous, murderous vessels in the hands of their infernal lord, Satan. Revelation 2:10 says the Synagogue of Satan will cast some Christians into prison and kill many others. Their evil plot to conquer the world by stealth and deceit will finally bring about a precarious *Hour of Temptation* for all mankind *(Revelation 3:10)*. So, why aren't pastors and evangelists today warning us to watch out for and beware of these imposter Jews of the Synagogue of Satan?

The riddle of those who say they are Jews but are not, and do lie may be explained by the fact that the men at the top tier of power in the Synagogue of Satan organization have been proven by many respected researchers to be *"Khazar Jews,"* also called *"Ashkenazi Jews."* The Khazars were a Turk-

Mongol people who lived centuries ago in the Kingdom of Khazaria, eventually to be integrated into the Russian Empire by the Czars. The King of the Khazars forced his citizens, upon penalty of death, to convert to Judaism. Later, after their takeover by hostile enemies, demographers and historians say that the Khazars migrated into Eastern Europe, especially to Poland, Lithuania, Romania, and Hungary.

There, in Europe, the Khazars—who said they were "Jews" and practiced a mystical and pagan form of Judaism—gathered in their own communities, keeping separate from those around them whom they classified as "Gentiles." The Khazar "Jews" were, in fact, themselves Gentiles, yet adopting the racist Jewish religion, they considered other Gentiles to be racial inferiors. The racial inferiority of Gentiles was taught to them in their Talmud.

Europe soon became populated by peoples who said they were Jews, who acculturated as Jews, who adopted and practiced the Babylonian Judaic Pharisaic Religion, but who *were not* real Jews. Most of these people have not a drop of Jewish blood in their bodies, yet they pretend to be "Jews." Many no doubt have bought into their own historical lie. Others know the truth, but attempt to conceal their true, non-Jew heritage to gain advantage since it pays to be a Jew.

To this day, the Ashkenazi Jews, the heirs of the Khazar genealogical lineage, shun DNA tests. They want no evidence produced that will prove they are *not* Jews. They continue to lie and say they are Jews.

In fact, an increasing number of DNA studies and analyses have been published over the past decade. In every case, it was scientifically established that a vast majority of the people alive today who say they are Jews have little or no DNA relationship to the ancient bloodline of the Israelites. One researcher has even reported that Arabs and Palestinians probably have a greater percentage of ancient Israelite blood flowing through their veins than today's modern-day "Jew."

It is as if the modern-day descendants of Attila the Hun, Genghis Khan, or Japan's World War II Emperor Hirohito were to falsely declare, with absolutely no proof or evidence to back up their contention, that they are "Jews", and the whole world were to foolishly accept their preposterous, juvenile and unscientific bloodline claims.

Why do these Jewish imposters insist, in the face of overwhelming evidence to the contrary, that they are "Jews?" Why do they falsely lay claim to being in the direct lineage of Israel's patriarchs, Abraham, Moses, Elijah, and others?

The reason is clear: FOR ADVANTAGE. When modern-day Israel was formed in 1948, the Khazar/Ashkenazi Jews took all the leadership roles in that fledgling nation. Men who lied and said they were Jews, but were not, soon were receiving billions of dollars in free foreign aid money from U.S.A. taxpayers and hundreds of millions more in reparations from a defeated German nation.

These Jewish imposters, moreover, garnered the sympathy and support of billions of deceived dupes around the world who feel guilty or who want to help Jewish *holocaust* victims—though few of the Khazars really ever were victims.

In effect, what we have here is a massive *Personality and Race Cult*, made up of false "Jews" who enthusiastically pretend they are God's Chosen People, the "apple" of His eye, but in reality are blasphemers of God, liars extraordinaire, and global scam artists! These, then, are the denizens of the hellish Synagogue of Satan, who are exposed so well in this book by Andrew Hitchcock.

Wherever those who say they are Jews have chosen to reside in the world today, they prosper and thrive.

In America this is doubly true. In his insightful book, *The*

Power of Israel in the United States, Professor James Petras documents the overwhelming control exercised over U.S. foreign and domestic policy by the Jewish Lobby and by Israel. Jews represent only about 2.2% of America's voter-age demographics. The basis for their power, says Petras, is Jewish wealth. In other words—*Money*.

"The basis of the (Jewish) Lobby's PAC power is rooted in the high proportion of Jewish families among the wealthiest families in the United States. According to *Forbes*, 25 to 30 percent of U.S. multimillionaires and billionaires are Jewish."

Due to their willingness to exercise this Money Power to advance their own race and its prospects, Petras writes, the Jews have established a "tyranny over the U.S."—a tyranny that, Petras warns, *"has grave consequences for world peace and war, the stability and unstability of the world economy, and for the future of democracy in the U.S."*

Petras, in his book, convincingly demonstrates the vile nature of the unseemly Jewish influence over the U.S. political establishment. The United States, because of unrelenting Jewish demands, has become the military and economic proxy of Israel in the Middle East and the globe, committing violence, torture, assassination, terrorism, robbery of resources, and thuggery on a grand scale. When the Jewish Power tell us to do it, we jump to go and do it. Even the horror of genocide is perpetrated if it is to the advantage of the Jews.

In effect, the United States has become a colony of Greater Israel. We, the people of America, act as the Jews' global bodyguard, fixer, and hit man. We, led by the Gentile puppets who slavishly do the bidding of the Jewish Money Masters, are global capos. On behalf of Jewish interests we are busy converting the entire world into one, giant concentration camp. We are the camp's guards and its executioners; the "Jews" are its commandants, and the people of planet earth are its inmates. At the mere whim of the Synagogue of Satan, the inmates are starved, worked to death, and discarded.

The best and brightest of the Gentiles are rewarded with grotesque entertainments and lustful transient pleasures. Until their usefulness is exhausted and then, they, too, are thrown off the deep end of a pier, dying of alcoholism, clogged arteries, Alzheimer's, and other diseases brought on by the debilitating pharmaceuticals sold by Jewish-owned corporate drug giants.

Please keep in mind that God is no respecter of persons, and that racial advantage has no part to play in God's heavenly Jerusalem. Indeed, contrary to the doctrines of devils spread by lying Zionist evangelicals, God does not distinguish between races in choosing a people for His name. *Galatians 3:28-29* is marvelous in dispelling satanic notions of racial superiority. God does not favor those who are "Jew" or those of any one race or ethnic heritage. Instead, the Bible invites men and women of every nation and race on earth to come and drink of Jesus' living water: *"And if ye be Christ's, then are ye Abraham's seed and heirs according to the promise."*

Paul perfectly explains the spiritual applications of this life-giving principle when he states that according to the Word of God, *"They which are the children of the flesh, these are not the children of God: but the children of the promise are counted for the seed" (Romans 9:8).*

What a wonderful thing! Regardless of a person's race or bloodline, and in spite of lowly physical or geographical origins, any man or woman can be elevated to the high and eternal status of God's Chosen. How is this amazing feat accomplished? Through faith in Jesus Christ alone, for it is the gift of God, a gift awarded not based on a man's racial heritage, but on the spiritual treasure that resides in his heart.

Tragically, today I find that many, indeed, almost the

whole majority of Jews, have bought into the lies of the Synagogue of Satan. Their xenophobic, though untrue, racial and national pride has overcome far too many Jews. Secular Jews and religious "Jews" alike have fallen in the trap. Believing the rabbis' lying doctrines, as elaborated in the poisonous, racially infused holy books of Judaism, the Talmud and the texts of the Kaballah, those who identify themselves as Jews often love to presume they are smarter, better, more spiritual, more divine than their fellows who are Gentiles.

These "Jews" may be privy to or may not even remotely understand the heinous plan and designs of the Sabbatian, satanic "Jews" of the Synagogue of Satan. Nevertheless, by flattery they have been deceived. So, they sit back and luxuriate and bask in the glow of their supposed racial blood superiority. They also acquiesce in the imperial designs of the butchers who run the fascist government of today's physical nation of Israel. They believe it when their rabbis tell them that as God's Chosen, their destiny is to rule the world and acquire all its wealth. They give monies to politicians and to Jewish causes that lead to violence and bloodshed for the beleaguered Palestinians and Arabs. After all, Arabs are thought to be inferior people. Many rabbis eagerly classify Arabs and other Gentiles as like unto insects, Goyim (cattle) at best, destined for the dung heap of history. *Long live the Jewish Super race!*

It is true that not every Jew expresses such deviant views. Yet, many "Jews" are silent. Inwardly, they crave the rabbinical and talmudic flattery heaped on them. They also realize that they gain advantage because they are "Jews," so they say and do nothing to prevent the Synagogue of Satan from advancing its goals. In truth, the silent are themselves complicit. Omission and commission are one and the same. And "not to decide" to do what is right *is* to decide to do what is wrong.

238 O TEXE MARRS

It has always been the case that the cowardly inactions of the "Silent Majority" lend power and credentials to the active Minority who rule. In the recent American war against the hapless, suffering citizens of Iraq, the U.S. Armed Forces have, according to a Johns Hopkins Medical University Study published in the respected *Lancet* medical journal, now massacred over 655,000 Iraqis. This gruesome statistic is of non-combatant, innocent men, women and children.

But watch out!—It is not only the military brass and the leaders in the Administration who are culpable in this genocidal crime. Every American citizen, by his inaction and failure to protest, is guilty of this mayhem and murder.

Likewise, every person who says, "I am a Jew" and who, being racially prejudiced and bigoted, tends to prefer his or her supposed racial tribe (Jew) to all others and proceeds to discriminate and mistreat the so-called inferior Gentiles (Goyim) is guilty of satanic crimes. This is especially the case for all those who are Zionists; all such people are guilty of membership in, and support for, the Synagogue of Satan. This includes Jewish bankers, corporate CEOs, educators, teachers, broadcasters—the whole kit and caboodle of people who say they are "Jews."

Virtually all Jews, by extension, are of the Synagogue of Satan. A Jew may say, "No, that cannot be. I did not vote for these evil men. I do not approve of their monstrous deeds. I just live my daily life in the pursuit of happiness and prosperity."

Do not be deceived. You are wrong. You *are* guilty. You may be silent, yet your inaction makes you as a willing accomplice in the crimes and designs of the Synagogue of Satan. You are a co-conspirator, and you *will* someday pay the full price for your heinous crimes, whether of omission or commission.

Is this a "collective guilt?" Yes, indeed it is and while man may frown on it, God has ordained it. Truly, all of mankind is under a collective curse due to the fall of Adam and Eve in the Garden. That is why man needs a redeemer, to redeem and deliver him from this curse. As for the Jews, Jesus Himself solemnly declared this prophecy.

> *"Fill ye up then the measure of your fathers. Ye serpents, ye generation (race) of vipers, how can ye escape the damnation of hell? ...That upon you may come all the righteous bloodshed upon the earth...*
>
> *Behold, your house is left unto you desolate."*
> *(Matthew 23: 32-38)*

Whether man likes it or not, Jesus Christ has placed a terrible, collective curse on the Jews. If a man, by his own tongue, identifies himself as a Jew, even if he lies in doing so, he unwisely places himself under this horrendous curse. He becomes, then, a cog in the terrible inhuman machine called the Synagogue of Satan. Yet, let it be known by all that every man and woman, Jew and Gentile, is offered liberty and a means of escape from the curse through faith in Jesus Christ our Lord. A curse may be collective or individual, but the blessings of salvation and deliverance are always tendered to individuals.

So as not to be misconstrued, I level this same warning and accusation against Gentiles. You Gentiles who suspect or know of the evil ways of the elite leaders of the Synagogue of Satan and do nothing to stop them—or worse, act as their accomplice—are equally guilty of their crimes. Thus, the Synagogue of Satan is made up not only of lying, blasphemous men and women who say they are Jews and are not, but also of Gentiles who collaborate with them. All are complicit and are serving Lucifer.

What is the ultimate goal of the Synagogue of Satan? Its goal is to corrupt mens' souls, destroy every independent government and enslave the world in a Luciferian dictatorship led by their own Despot King. The method they employ as they proceed in this endeavor is to cause chaos, followed by their own well-designed establishment of order: *Ordo Ab Chao*. Cyclically, perpetually played out on the world scene, they cause wars and revolutions and foster economic chaos and social instability. Chaos is their engine of progress until, eventually, all of mankind is so exhausted people everywhere are expected to desperately cry out for a World Authority to finally bring in order and global peace. But for the evil-doers who say they are Jews there truly is no peace to be had. Only a police state with absolute slavery for all mankind will satisfy them.

Why are these evil-doers so determined to wreak havoc, to work bloodshed and to demolish the earth to bring about their long-sought, vain-glorious *"Jewish Utopia?"* I do not blink to state to you clearly and in no uncertain terms that the worst of these wicked perverts are Luciferians. The people at the very top of the Synagogue of Satan are possessed by devils. Their plot is of biblical proportions. It is also of intergenerational character. The same demons who yesterday infested Mayer Rothschild, Napoleon, Marx, and Lenin today work inside the human shells of 21st century disciples. Since the day of Luciferian deception in the Garden of Eden and the murder of righteous Abel by Satan's Cain, these partisans of hell have labored.

Their more recent incarnations have produced the horrors of World Wars I and II, and the so-called Cold War and its many conflicts. Now, through their aggression and wars in the

Middle East, they threaten to annihilate and engulf the world in the nuclear nightmare of World War III. The death and misery will never stop until Christ returns again.

The Synagogue of Satan will steadily deceive, slander, kill and plot until the end comes. They have no other choice. The devil and his fallen angels eons ago rolled the dice, figuratively speaking, and lost. They foolishly rebelled and now must pay the full penalty. So, too, will all those who ally themselves with today's devil-led Synagogue of Satan.

Someday, all who ally themselves with the Synagogue of Satan, including those who attempt to remain aloof and choose to remain silent, will be forced to grovel at the very feet of those whom the Synagogue of Satan have so viciously and cruelly robbed, persecuted, and killed.

> *"Behold, I will make them of the synagogue of Satan, which say they are Jews, and are not, but do lie; behold, I will make them to come and worship before thy feet, and to know that I have loved thee."*
> *(Revelation 3:9)*

INDEX

ABOUT THE AUTHOR

Well-known author of the #1 national bestseller, *Dark Secrets of The New Age*, Texe Marrs has written 46 books for such major publishers as Simon & Schuster, John Wiley, Prentice Hall/Arco, McGraw-Hill, and Dow Jones-Irwin. His books have sold millions of copies. He is one of the world's foremost symbologists and is a first-rate scholar of ancient history and Mystery religions.

Texe Marrs was assistant professor of aerospace studies, teaching American defense policy, strategic weapons systems, and related subjects at the University of Texas at Austin for five years. He has also taught international affairs, political science, and psychology for two other universities. A graduate *summa cum laude* from Park College, Kansas City, Missouri, he earned his Master's degree at North Carolina State University.

As a career USAF officer (now retired), he commanded communications-electronics and engineering units. He holds a number of military decorations including the Vietnam Service Medal and Presidential Unit Citation, and has served in Germany, Italy, and throughout Asia.

President of RiverCrest Publishing in Austin, Texas, Texe Marrs is a frequent guest on radio and TV talk shows throughout the U.S.A. and Canada. His monthly newsletter, *Power of Prophecy*, is distributed around the world, and he is heard globally on his popular, international shortwave and internet radio program, *Power of Prophecy*. His articles and research are published regularly on his exclusive websites: *powerofprophecy. com* and *conspiracyworld.com*.

FOR OUR NEWSLETTER

Texe Marrs offers a free sample copy of his newsletter focusing on world events, false religion, and secret societies, cults, and the occult challenge to Christianity. If you would like to receive this newsletter, please write to:

Power of Prophecy
1708 Patterson Road
Austin, Texas 78733

You may also e-mail your request to:
customerservice1@powerofprophecy.com

FOR OUR WEBSITE

Texe Marrs' newsletter is published free monthly on our websites. These websites have descriptions of all Texe Marrs' books, and are packed with interesting, insight-filled articles, videos, breaking news, and other information. You also have the opportunity to order an exciting array of books, tapes, and videos through our online Catalog and Sales Stores. Visit our websites at:

www.powerofprophecy.com
www.conspiracyworld.com

OUR SHORTWAVE RADIO PROGRAM

Texe Marrs' international radio program, *Power of Prophecy*, is broadcast weekly on shortwave radio throughout the United States and the world. *Power of Prophecy* can be heard on WWCR at 4.840 Saturdays at 7:00 p.m. Central Time. A repeat of the program is aired on Sunday nights at 9:00 p.m. Central Time. You may also listen to *Power of Prophecy* 24/7 on websites *powerofprophecy.com* and *conspiracyworld.com*.

MORE RESOURCES FOR YOU

Books:

Conspiracy of the Six-Pointed Star—Eye Opening Revelations and Forbidden Knowledge About Israel, the Jews, Zionism, and the Rothschilds, by Texe Marrs (432 pages) $30.00

Codex Magica—Secret Signs, Mysterious Symbols, and Hidden Codes of the Illuminati, by Texe Marrs (624 pages) $40.00

Conspiracy World—A Truthteller's Compendium of Eye-Opening Revelations and Forbidden Knowledge (432 pages) $30.00

Mysterious Monuments—Encyclopedia of Secret Illuminati Designs, Masonic Architecture, and Occult Places, by Texe Marrs (624 pages) $40.00

Videos:

Architectural Colossus—Mysterious Monuments Enshroud the World With Magic and Seduction (DVD) $30.00

Face to Face With the Devil—Close Encounters With Unexpected Evil (DVD) $30.00

The Sun at Midnight—Pyramids of Mystery, Temples of Blood (DVD) $30.00

Cauldron of Abaddon—**"From Jerusalem and Israel Flow a Torrent of Satanic Evil and Mischief Endangering the Whole World"** (DVD) $30.00

Thunder Over Zion—**Illuminati Bloodlines and the Secret Plan for A Jewish Utopia and a New World Messiah** (DVD) $30.00

Secret Societies and the Illuminati (DVD) $25.00

Illuminati Mystery Babylon—**The Hidden Elite of Israel, America, and Russia, and Their Quest for Global Dominion** (DVD) $30.00

ALL PRICES INCLUDE SHIPPING AND HANDLING
Visa/Mastercard/Discover Accepted

To order, phone 1-800-234-9673,
or send check or money order to:

Power of Prophecy
1708 Patterson Road,
Austin, Texas 78733

Check Out These Web Sites for more invaluable
books, videos, audiotapes,
and for breaking news and informative articles:

www.powerofprophecy.com
www.conspiracyworld.com

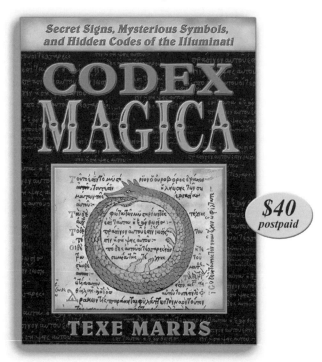